HELPING YOURSELF WITH

THE POWER OF GNOSTIC MAGIC

HELPING YOURSELF WITH THE POWER OF GNOSTIC MAGIC

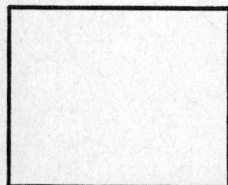

Al G. Manning

Parker Publishing Company, Inc., West Nyack, New York

This book is a reference work based on research by
the author. The opinions expressed herein are not
necessarily those of or endorsed by the Publisher.

© 1979, *by*

PARKER PUBLISHING COMPANY, INC.

West Nyack, N.Y.

Library of Congress Cataloging in Publication Data

Manning, Al G
    Helping yourself with the power of gnostic magic.

    1. Success. 2. Magic. I. Title.
BJ1611.2.M329   131'.32   79-13447
ISBN 0-13-386698-X

Printed in the United States of America

DEDICATION

I happily dedicate this book to you, in anticipation of my special satisfaction from learning that you have used it to make a more wonderful life for yourself.

And here also special thanks to Fay, my loving wife, who lived the book with me and put up with the many inconveniences and esoteric experiments at all hours of the day and night, and who typed the manuscript as well.

How Gnostic Magic Can Make You Rich

If I handed you a golden key to the doorway to fulfillment of your most cherished dreams and desires, would you put it on a shelf and say, "I'll get around to it later"? This book is your golden key, and I urge you to promise yourself that you will keep it with you and give its enjoyable work maximum priority until it has opened ALL the doors for you.

Life is a game of "more." EVERYBODY wants *more* of something, you can be quite sure that to this there are NO exceptions. And so this book is for YOU because its purpose is to show you in simple, easy steps how to get more of everything you want. You will fulfill your desires with *less* struggle and work than you are doing now, because your *magic* is fun to do and it will replace much of the effort and work of the past. Whether your desire is for money, love, health, riches, companionship, spiritual growth—or ALL of these and more—it is attainable through the Gnostic Magical practices I have set forth for you in this book. You will find every part of this magic both easy and fun, with every step bringing you fresh and wonderful rewards for your striving. Gnostic Magic has plenty for all. Let's peek at a few examples of results that others have reported.

7

**HOW THESE GNOSTIC MAGICAL PRACTICES
HAVE HELPED OTHERS**

After his first use of the Gnostic Ritual for Effectiveness
(page 28), J.G. reported completing a three-day job in less than
six hours; and a slight variation of the same first ritual saved
S.Z.'s business and allowed him to buy out a completely
intractable partner (page 30).

Charlie G. had been out of a job for six months. He used
the sacrifice ritual from Chapter 2 one evening and the next
morning, and by nightfall had a job in a better position than
the one he had lost (page 38). D.C. used the ritual of joy from
Chapter 2 and dissolved all opposition to her marriage to a
loving and very wealthy man (page 44).

Jessie G. used the protection Gnosis from Chapter 3 to
dissolve a terrible conflict with her supervisor and get a merit
raise with a supervisor's approval (page 50).

M.H. used the Gnostic Money Manifesting Ritual for 11
days and got a $10,000-a-year raise and promotion to plant
manager—after 15 years in the same lower job (page 66). And
B.C. used it to win two Keno jackpots in the same day (page
66).

Lilly S. had broken up with her long-time lover. She used
the Gnostic Love/Friendship Ritual after a couple of months.
Result: he called up and they were married (page 78). Dorothy
S. used the ritual for friendship with the small creatures and
developed a rapport with a bluejay who gave her tips on the
races. She won $1,200 on her first trip to the track (page 83).

Jerimiah I. used the Gnostic Perfect Health Ritual to cure
his bad back and slept straight through the night for the first
time in 14 years (page 93), and C.C. used it to easily pass
kidney stones the doctors could not believe she passed that
way (page 94).

Bob L. used the Gnostic Exorcism Rite to effortlessly take
himself from 360 pounds to 180 pounds in just six months of
perfect health (page 121), and he got a nice promotion as a
happy side effect.

And these are just a few typical results from only the first half of the book; it gets more powerful in the second half—read on and see for yourself.

THIS GNOSTIC MAGIC HAS BEEN RESURRECTED FOR YOU OUT OF THE DISTANT PAST

History records the ancient Greek, Pythagoras, as the founder of the order of ritual magicians who became known as the Gnostics. Plato was another practitioner of these powerful magical rites, and later Gnostics were often called Neo-Platonists. And the magic blended so well with Christianity that the Gnostics were an important sect of the early Christian Church, at least through the time of Basilides of Alexandria. With the burning of the library of Alexandria and later persecution of the ceremonial magicians, most of the material of this book was lost to mankind. But by a technique of viewing the events of the past, which we will also give you in this book, these powerful practices have been brought back for you. I had plenty of help from the unseen side of life in bringing this through for you because its time has come—the time has come at last for human beings to learn to make their way in this world comfortably and happily, using magic to multiply their good and so multiply the total good of mankind. I do not offer you something for nothing—but I have set out for you an easy-to-implement magical program that will give you control over the forces of change and so the *power* to change any and every facet of your life.

Nothing can be held back from you as you joyously master the simple principles and practices given in this book. Success, health, happiness, love, fulfillment, prestige, and all the perquisites of the good life await your enjoyable application of the Gnostic Magical principles. But let's spend no more time in idle chatter; turn right to the first chapter and start to claim YOUR good NOW!

Al G. Manning

Table of Contents

7. DEFEAT THE EVIL EYE OR PSYCHIC ATTACK WITH GNOSTIC POWER ... 101

HELPING YOURSELF WITH

THE POWER OF GNOSTIC MAGIC

Become a Practical Gnostic Magician—and Start Living!

You hold in your hand the key to the secrets of the universe and the power to bring the desires of your heart into living reality. You will find it all set out for you in the pages of this book, so approach your reading with zest and enthusiasm. Nothing can stand in your way or hold you back because we will arm you with the ultimate secret weapon, KNOWLEDGE of how to harness the primordial forces and energies of nature to cause change under *your* direction. Big or little changes are all the same to the primordial energies; they will work without reservation or hesitation *every time* you pull the appropriate trigger. It is the special knowledge of how, when and where to pull the right trigger that we will call the GNOSIS, and you, as the one who has the knowledge, will be the GNOSTIC.

WHAT AND WHY IS A GNOSTIC?

The word *gnostic* has the same root as the more common word *gnosis*, which means to know. Thus *gnostic* quite literally means *one who knows*. The GNOSTICS as such in history look to the great Greek philosopher and mathematician, Pythagoras, as their founder, and trace the evolution of their magical doctrines on through Plato until they became an important part of Christianity in the first and second centuries. Later, as happened in so many of the early sects, their magic was so good that the purists in the organized church outlawed its practice and the Gnostics became one more underground sect, so secret that the order disappeared into the fog of the past. In a later chapter we will show you how to penetrate deeply into the secrets of even the distant past, but for now let's just explain that it was exactly in this manner that the material of this book was resurrected from its timeless grave and translated into modern language to be most useful to YOU.

Why should *you* be interested in these ancient Gnostic secrets? For only one reason: TO MAKE THEM WORK FOR YOU TO IMPROVE, UPLIFT AND POSITIVELY CHANGE ANY AND ALL AREAS OF YOUR LIFE. To know even a little of these ancient secrets is to see the universe in a completely new light, and thus to become one who knows—a GNOSTIC. And this is the proper path for a reasoning being; after all, knowledge of "how to" is the exact opposite of blind faith. When you know the laws of electricity, it is not blind faith that turns on a switch and expects to get light. And if the light does not come on, you don't worry that "somebody up there doesn't like me" but you simply check fuses, connections and the bulb itself with the certainty that when you have satisfied all of the physical laws, the light must come on at the flip of your switch.

I have been called a magician because I cause a fluorescent tube to light up without any wires connected to it. But no one would call that magic when they understand that I am simply using the tube as an electrical field detector to see if my strong tesla coil is tuned properly. This is merely a positive application of the laws of electricity, and the difference between *that* certainty and *your* certainty in using the principles of Gnostic Magic is only that the laws of Gnostic Magic are known to so few people. So just as I cause my fluorescent tube to give off light with no wires attached, you will apply your Gnosis to get consistently magnificent results—and for these manifestations you will accept the appellation "Magician" because it is easier than giving a detailed explanation of the magical laws. Be ready to call yourself a GNOSTIC or CEREMONIAL MAGICIAN as we unfold the basics for you in the rest of this chapter, then add the fine points in the balance of this book. My challenge to you is TRY IT AND WIN! Then you will USE it forever, whether you "believe in it" or not.

KNOWLEDGE OF "HOW TO" (GNOSIS) IS UNBEATABLE POWER

Back in the 1930s when I was growing up, there was a favorite old bromide that went, "The man who knows *how* will always have a job—working for the man who knows *why*." But the second half of our 20th century changed all that—and good old "American know-how" became the watchword. Indeed, we find the situation quite reversed now, with the research man who knows WHY often going with hat in hand to plead for his budget to the corporate president who is the man who knows HOW to get things done.

So we will stress the "how to," and occasionally hint at the theory. After you are RICH, COMFORTABLE AND WELL LOVED there will be plenty of time to indulge in epistemology, theory, "why," and all those good things. But first let's get the creature comforts and wherewithal to buy back enough of our time to spend on those or your other pet intellectual pursuits. So for NOW, let's put the emphasis where it will help you the most, and look for the KNOWLEDGE of HOW TO that will bring you the most immediate power and tangible benefits. And this surely leads us to the first of the GNOSTIC MAGICAL TRUTHS.

POLARITY AND THE PAIRS OF OPPOSITES— HOW TO MAKE THEM WORK FOR YOU

The Gnostics developed a unique and most practical set of ideas based on a true understanding of the pairs of opposites. The physical analogy is the north and south poles of magnetism, or the positive and negative poles of electricity; one cannot exist without the other. But in another sense we see for instance one pole that seems to have an excess of electrons which therefore try to flow out to reach the other pole which has a deficiency. With this for our model we can look at the key pair of Gnostic opposites—EFFECTIVENESS and its opposite pole INEFFECTIVENESS. In this sense effectiveness is the *energy*, and its opposite is properly thought of as *lack of or absence of effectiveness*, even as we now recognize darkness as merely the absence of the energy of light.

This makes it easy to recognize the basic principle of Gnostic Magic: *Identify with and apply the positive energy to bring about your desired change, and it will be opposed only by the negative opposite, which is nothing but an absence of power.*

We will be primarily concerned with nine special pairs of opposites that make up the power structure of Gnostic Magic. Some of the terms are not totally described by just one word, so in those cases I have added an explanatory word or two in parentheses:

Number	POSITIVE POLE (energy)	opposed by	NEGATIVE POLE (absence of energy)
9	Organization		Disorganization
8	Loyalty (receptivity)		Disloyality (unreceptive)
7	Unattachment (a whole being: spiritual power)		Attachment (clinging to; incomplete)
6	Awareness (communication; observation)		Unawareness (a clod)
5	Givingness (love)		Withholding (stingy; fear)
4	Strength (courage)		Weakness (indecision)
3	Effectiveness		Ineffectiveness
2	Light (intelligence)		Darkness (stupidity)
1	Attraction (attractiveness; physical power)		Repulsion (ugliness; frustration)

The exoteric Gnostic teaching was a God higher than the lesser deities of the time, including Jehovah, Baal and all the rest. This God manifested as the power pole we call *effectiveness*, and was called *Abraxas*. Abraxas is pure principle and in turn manifests through its principal representative, *Ishtar*. (Those of you who have read my *Magic of New Ishtar Power* will recognize here the beginning of the unfolding of the next level of power.) On the practical, magical level (the esoteric or inner teaching), we find effectiveness left to Ishtar with the Godhead, Abraxas, being better understood as ORGANIZATION.

In this sense of the word, organization is everything—the universe is considered to be simply a *thought* of Abraxas: *thought organized in time is energy, while thought organized in space is matter*; and we already know that matter can be converted to energy by man's intervention or by natural processes such as the atomic reactions that provide the energy of our sun.

But all this would be idle metaphysical speculation if we could not harness the knowledge to make our lives more comfortable, affluent and meaningful NOW and in the future. We will assume that we have laid enough theoretical groundwork for the moment, and go on to our first practical applications.

HOW TO SET THE STAGE FOR THE GNOSTIC RITUAL FOR EFFECTIVENESS

Whether it be the "stage" or "ceremonial" type, the word *magic* carries a strong connotation of awe and enthusiasm. And indeed *enthusiasm* is the closest one-word description we can give of the *power of effective Gnostic or ceremonial magic*. Enthusiasm flows merrily along, overwhelming or bypassing all obstacles to its happy fulfillment. Make this the keynote of all your work with this book. Attack your magical work with zest, gusto and enthusiasm, caring not too much for literal or nit-picking accuracy, but entering wholeheartedly into the SPIRIT of the work. As you make this your standard approach you will quickly see why I state as a natural law: *The life of the Gnostic Magician becomes one happy experience after another*.

This will give you a ready yardstick with which to measure the effectiveness of your magical work in advance— the more relaxed and full of sheer joy you find yourself at the conclusion of any ritual or magical work, the more power you got worked into it, so the greater its probability of manifestation.

Now let's talk specifics of preparation. You will need a place to work. A small table with a vanity mirror is best, but remember all the way through our work, your *enthusiasm* will make up for any lack of space, privacy or equipment. Those of you who have read one or more of my other books will know that you can use the altar area or quiet place you set up that time. Over the years I have made minor additions to my personal altar setup, but it is basically the same as the small table and mirror I started with in 1948. I always suggest candles (two tapers and a seven-day candle that burns constantly throughout your rituals and your absence—if it is possible for you), perfume oils and incense because they add 10 to 20% to the power; but make do with what is at hand in the short run. It is always better to try NOW with no equipment or props than to wait for a more propitious time which undoubtedly would never arrive anyway. And your initial results will encourage you to add more of the niceties.

On the personal level let us begin by stating that the most important thing you will ever study is *yourself*. Begin at once to make more careful mental notes of what stimuli turn you on in a positive manner. What are the conditions, situations and things that make you feel good and fill you with enthusiasm? It is good to make a long mental list, so regardless of your beginning mood, you have a set of tricks to get joy and enthusiasm surging around you. For our opening efforts, bring all the peace, zest, enthusiasm and joy you can muster to your chosen ritual place and let's have a go at the first concrete step to your richer, fuller life.

THE GNOSTIC RITUAL FOR EFFECTIVENESS

It is natural that we should begin with a ritual for effectiveness—it will make you more effective in all the other work of this book as well as in your normal daily life. And it will give you your first taste of the tremendous power that you are about to have at your disposal. The power is contacted best by a ritual of sacrifice, but this one is the kind you will most gladly offer. You will see both the symbology and the practical value of sacrificing your ineffectiveness to Ishtar and your disorganization to Abraxas, and receiving in turn their special power of effectiveness and organization.

The simple preparation for the ritual is to write on a small piece of paper: "I willingly and lovingly offer the sacrifice of my ineffectiveness to Ishtar and my disorganization to Abraxas. And I gladly accept your gifts of effectiveness and organization, and pledge their efficient use in improving all areas of my life." Then sign it with your normal signature.

Take your piece of paper to your prepared ritual place, along with a heavy ashtray or a saucer lined with aluminum foil which can safely hold the paper while it burns. Light your candles and incense and apply your perfume oil to your brow, throat and heart. (If you do not choose to use candles, incense and oil, it's all right, but do follow through with the idea of using them in your imagination to set the mood of awe and zest.)

Hold your piece of paper between your palms comfortably in front of you as you visualize a shaft of bright white LIGHT shining directly down on you as if there were a searchlight in the ceiling above your head. Feel the warmth and love in the LIGHT as it beams down on you and just bask in the loving glow for a few moments. Now read aloud the sacrificial declaration from your paper three times *with feeling*, then hold it to the candle flame (or the flame of a match) until a corner catches fire, repeat the declaration again and drop the burning paper safely into the ashtray. As you watch the paper

being completely consumed by the flame, you should sense a definite sensation of great power. Sit quietly and soak it up while you remain alert to ideas and practical suggestions that will be "popped" into your mind.

But don't be disappointed if you think that nothing happened; there can be wonderful results anyway, as this report from an accountant friend of mine, J.G., clearly shows:

"Thank you for suggesting that I start my new year with the Gnostic Ritual for Effectiveness! I tried it on New Year's evening and nothing much seemed to happen. I forgot about it until my experience the next day. I tackled the balancing of a big payroll for the quarterly and annual reports and W2s which I expected to be about a three-day job. Everything I did came out perfectly the first time—it was quite uncanny! And I completed the three-day job in slightly less than six hours! Just to see if it was 'coincidence' I repeated the ritual that evening, and sure enough I had another day of really magnificent effectiveness. I'm hooked on this simple ritual—I expect to use it for the rest of my working life at least."

And from E.M. in Nigeria, West Africa came this happy report: "To my great astonishment, a problem which had withstood all my ingenuity for more than three years—I repeat, for more than three years—was solved for me on Friday morning without my soliciting for it, after just two evenings of performing your Gnostic Ritual for Effectiveness. Who will say it is just a coincidence? If a coincidence, what has been preventing the coincidence from happening before now? I tender unto Almighty God, the Creator of the Universe and the Planter of all Mysteries, my grateful thanks, also to the Elemental Spirits, to the wonderful spirit friends, and to you, Al, for making these mysteries available to me and others through your wonderful work."

NOW YOU ARE A GNOSTIC—HOW TO HARNESS YOUR INTRODUCTION TO GNOSTIC MAGIC FOR IMMEDIATE BENEFITS

Once you have used the Gnostic Ritual for Effectiveness and obtained your first taste of positive results, *you are a*

Gnostic—you are indeed ONE WHO KNOWS that the magic works. Accept your new title happily and begin applying your new Gnosis to the sticky problems that have been bothering you.

The same simple ritual for effectiveness can be easily adapted to more specific problem solving by adding one short line to your written affirmation. Again write it by hand on a small piece of paper, as follows:

"I willingly and lovingly offer the sacrifice of my ineffectiveness to Ishtar and my disorganization to Abraxas. I gladly accept your gifts of effectiveness and organization and pledge their efficient use in improving all areas of my life. And I ask your help in focusing this great power to bring a positive and happy solution to my problem of _____. [*Here you fill in a statement of the problem in the shortest, simplest and most positive terms you can*.] My heartfelt thanks for your wonderful help." And again sign the paper with your normal signature.

This simple variation of the ritual can accomplish magnificent results for you. Let's share the experience of Phyllis S. for example. Phyllis was "madly in love" with her husband's best friend. They had been meeting secretly for six years, but could not bring themselves to seek freedom to marry because each felt an obligation to the friend and spouse and did not want to hurt the other parties. And, of course, there were children involved on both sides. Phyllis used the ritual for effectiveness, and we will let her finish the story: "I used the Gnostic Ritual for Effectiveness with the variation of asking for help to focus the power to bring a happy way to be with my lover, yet bring hurt to no one. It seemed like a very tall order, but somehow I felt very good doing the ritual. My determination was to do it every night until something happened, and I was *amazed* at how short a time I had to wait. On the evening of the fourth day, my husband asked me to sit down and talk. He told me that he had not wanted to hurt me, but he could stand it no longer—he was deeply in love with his best friend's wife. There was *actually* a corollary to my love for that same best friend. When I realized he was serious, I said it would be wonderful for the four of us to sit down and work out the happy details. You may have heard of miserable results of two couples exchanging marriage partners, but I guarantee that this case is magnificent. The four of us are all closer and better friends, there is no more guilt, we are all wonderfully fulfilled—and the children adjusted to the change beautifully. It sounds like a storybook or something, but it *happened*. My special thanks to Abraxas, Ishtar, and you, Al. It's wonderful!''

H.D. had this to report: "I used the Gnostic Ritual for Effectiveness with the variation of asking help to focus the power to get a job. Next morning I picked up the phone and inquired about work in Alaska. I was dispatched the next morning. I have since learned from the Union business agent that there were 1,500 names on the waiting list. Then they were cutting back on our hours and apparently about to terminate me. I used the ritual again and asked for help to keep me working. The next day they raised our working hours from 15 to 18 and four days later to 19. I have since learned that I will be the last of my skill to be cut. The Gnostic Magic is great!''

THE POTENTIAL OF YOUR GNOSTIC MAGIC IS UNLIMITED

This far we have looked at really good results from early attempts to harness just two of the pairs of opposites. You already know that there are nine key sets, so we have only begun to get a minute taste of the full power. I want to defer development of the next bit of theory until our next chapter; then we will look more fully at the mechanism of opposites and how even this powerful set of tools is but one small part of a much bigger whole. But permit me to jump the gun just enough to give you a taste of the next level of power. This is explained in a report from S.Z., which you will understand completely after the work of our next chapter:

"I was at my wit's end, to say the least. My business partner had become completely impossible and it was obvious that he was about to bring the business to bankruptcy—and me with it. I had tried sweetness and light, ranting and raving, cojoling, lecturing, even threatened to commit suicide, but the man just kept on making things worse. As you suggested I added a third opposite to the Gnostic effectiveness ritual like this: 'I willingly and lovingly offer the sacrifice of my frustration to Nergal, my ineffectiveness to Ishtar and my disorganization to Abraxas. I gladly accept your gifts of power, effectiveness and organization and pledge their efficent use in improving all areas of my life. And I ask your help in focusing the great power to save my business.' I actually felt my frustration leave me as I earnestly offered it in sacrifice to Nergal, but that was about all I felt that night. But it was obviously enough! Next morning, my belligerent partner came in like a pussycat and offered to sell me his share of the business on completely acceptable terms. We shook on it and he left in peace. Now all will be well, thanks to the Gnostic Magic."

If you have not already done so, stop *right now* and perform the Gnostic Ritual for Effectiveness, and promise yourself to do it for at least three days in a row. But do it once NOW so you will have its feeling and effectiveness working for you as we dig into the powerful work that awaits you in our next chapter.

GNOSTIC MAGIC MIND JOGGERS

1. This book gives you the knowledge you need to harness the primordial forces and energies of nature, causing change under *YOUR* direction. You will learn to accomplish anything you really desire by using Gnostic Magic.
2. The power secrets of Gnostic Magic were lost in the fog of time, but are resurrected for you here by a process of examining the past that you will also learn in a later chapter.
3. You will learn to apply your Gnosis to uplift, improve and positively change all areas of your life.
4. The first principle of Gnostic Magic is the harnessing of the positive power of the pairs of opposites—to let them work for you against a total lack of opposition.

5. Get familiar with the nine key sets of opposites to be ready to harness their power.
6. Use the Gnostic Ritual for Effectiveness to gain super effectivess for the rest of your work with this book as well as for your "normal" living.
7. You can apply the extra power of the variation of the effectiveness ritual for immediate help in specific problems.
8. Do the ritual for effectiveness at least once, then you are ready for the more powerful work of our next chapter.

Command Powerful Spirit Entities of the Gnosis for Immediate Help

I trust that your first taste of the power of Gnostic Magic was delicious. Now let's add enough understanding to lift you out of the "beginner's luck" category and make you something of a competent Magician. We will begin with an overview of the more nearly complete system in table form (see following page); then we will explain its meaning and use in detail.

Those who are familiar with my *Magic of New Ishtar Power* will recognize that we worked with a somewhat similar table in its second chapter, but here the emphasis is shifted to bring YOU a much more complete understanding and command of the powers and energies. Basically, the positive energy poles are regulated by the energy transformer personalities to bring the necessary amounts and frequencies of energy into your life expression through psychic energy centers or chakras in your emotional or astral beingness. The Gnostic Magic Power Structure Table shows the areas of manifestation governed by each energy transformer personality. Let's reach for the first handles on the power by introducing ourselves to the individual personalities.

THE GNOSTIC MAGIC POWER STRUCTURE

Number	Positive Energy Pole	Energy Transformer Personality	Luminary	Psychic Center (chakra)	Color	Governed Area of Human Manifestation
9	Organization	Abraxas	—	—	—	Pure principle
8	Receptivity	Isis	Moon	Risen Kundalini	White or Red-Violet	Enlightenment, cosmic consciousness, Satori, Samadhi, total oneness
7	Unattachment	Bast	Saturn	Crown	Violet	Spiritual power, lessons understood, fulfillment
6	Awareness	Thoth	Mercury	Brow	Indigo	Communication in all forms, psychic ability, spirit contact
5	Creativity	Marduk	Jupiter	Throat	Blue	Creativity, controlled change, healing, thought-form control
4	Strength	Osiris	Earth	Heart	Green	Love, givingness, growth, prosperity, wealth
3	Effectiveness	Ishtar	Venus	Solar Plexus	Yellow	Aspiration, intuition, material power
2	Light	Ra	Sun	Spleen	Orange	Positive will, mental clarity, power of intelligent thought
1	Attraction	Nergal	Mars	Root	Red	Physical vitality and healing, personal magnetism, sex drive

THE ENERGY TRANSFORMER PERSONALITIES

NERGAL (rhymes with *gurgle*) controls the energies of attraction that are associated with your animal magnetism, physical vitality (thus healing or regenerative powers), and sex drive. In astrology this energy is associated with the planet Mars. This is your most potent power for manifestations of a purely physical nature and must be present in useful form to attract the opportunity and wherewithal of any material accomplishment. In standard occult terminology, Nergal works through your root center, the point near the base of your spine. As you learn to bring in larger portions of this energy, you will notice that all people and animals tend to treat you with greater interest and respect than before.

RA (as in college yell—*rah,rah,rah*) brings you the special Light energies of positive will, clarity of mind and thought, and the ability to study well and make clear mental pictures. In astrology this is associated with the energy of the sun. Ra works through what is commonly called your spleen center to bring this extra mental power to you. Unlike the physical spleen, the spleen chakra is located along your spine about halfway between the root center and the solar plexus. All effective scholarship and intelligent thought requires this energy, and you will find that a clear flowing spleen center will bring you much extra insight and general mental ability.

ISHTAR (with the accent on the first syllable) brought me a lot of static from scholarly types when he chose to manifest to me in male form (since Ishtar was a classic Babylonian female diety), but it has certainly all been worth it. Ishtar focuses the effectiveness energy through your solar plexus chakra to enhance your aspiration, intuition and material effectiveness. And you will find this energy a special key to contact and use all the others. A clear flowing solar plexus center will open the doors of material and financial progress to you in ways beyond your fondest hopes, and give you effective, loving contact with all the other energy transformer personalities.

OSIRIS (long *O* and it rhymes with the flower, *iris*) focuses the earthy energy through your heart center, bringing you the strength from which you can truly love and give and grow. We associate the chakra with love as givingness, and so quite equally with prosperity and wealth. The energy partakes of the rich productiveness of the earth itself and can best be understood in that manner. In combination with the Ishtar energy, the clear flowing heart center will assure you of a life of loving luxury.

MARDUK (accent on the *mar* which rhymes with *car*, then *duk* which sounds like duke as in royalty), is the master magician of the group, controlling the energy of creativity through your throat chakra. This is the broad use of creativity which includes directed and controlled change of all kinds: thus healing, all of the arts, and inventiveness of all kinds. In astrological terms this is the Jupiter energy well seasoned with the power of Uranus. A clear flowing throat center will inevitably bring you the most creative solutions to your old problems and innovative approaches to your new ones.

THOTH (rhymes with broth) directs the special energy of awareness through your brow chakra. In astrological terms we find here the energy of Mercury, the messenger of the gods. All forms of communication are enhanced by the clear flow of the brow chakra energy; not just writing and speaking, but the intuitional faculties and all your psychic and spirit communication work as well.

BAST (rhymes with *last*) is the patron of the uppermost or crown chakra, focusing the vast spiritual power that we try to describe with the word *unattachment* to bring the most positive progress into your life. Bast is associated with the astrological energy of Saturn, but don't quake or hide at this one; Saturn is the great teacher and bill collector, who *always* sees to it that you get what you deserve. Make peace with yourself and join me in saying: "I love to see Saturn (or Bast) at work because she brings me what I deserve, and I deserve only the BEST." A clear flowing crown chakra will certainly play a large role in bringing you your highest good at every moment of your life experience.

ISIS (accent on the first syllable, which rhymes with *ice*; second syllable is *is*) and Abraxas (*A* as in *ah*, *brax* to rhyme with *axe*, *as* pronounced as *us*; accent on the *axe*) do not work through specific psychic centers of your body but rather add power, meaning and beauty to the whole of your beingness. When you have experienced your personal enlightenment, the full import of the magnificence that is here for you will be yours, and you will understand the true meaning of the brotherhood of all beings and your oneness with all that is.

PRACTICAL FUNCTIONS OF THE CHAKRAS
AND HOW TO GET INSTANT HELP FROM AN
ENERGY TRANSFORMER PERSONALITY

The last example of our opening chapter hinted at how easy it is to get instant help from the energy transformer personalities by a simple variation of the Gnostic Ritual of Sacrifice. You have only to define your problem in terms of which chakra is not bringing you the power you need for immediate success. Then offer the negative manifestation as a sacrifice to the related energy transformer personality in the sacrifice ritual, and accept the positive power in return. Note that with this we ALWAYS also offer our ineffectiveness and disorganization to Ishtar and Abraxas to assure the success of the ritual. A few simple examples here will be the easiest way to bring you a full understanding of the process:

M.S. was a high school student taking her first semester of German. Her mid-term grade was a miserable F, and she was very worried about this perhaps delaying her graduation, and certainly making it harder to be accepted in a good college. She used the sacrifice ritual in this form: "I lovingly and willingly offer the sacrifice of my confusion to Ra, my ineffectiveness to Ishtar and my disorganization to Abraxas. I gladly accept your gifts of mental clarity, effectiveness and organization and I ask your help in focusing the power to make me a better student, and particularly to be a good student of German. My heartfelt thanks to you all." Let's let

M.S. continue the story in her own words: "I used the Gnostic Sacrifice Ritual the first time just at bedtime. Next morning, I felt relaxed and almost eager to go to school. In my German class, I actually answered a question correctly—for just about the first time. The day went very well, so I repeated the ritual at bedtime again. To summarize, I used the ritual every night for a week, then tapered off to once a week (on Sunday at bedtime). You'll be proud of me, and so am I. The mid-term F in German actually became an A (the instructor said in view of my improvement, he could quite properly ignore the first half of the semester's work), and I wound up with four A's and a B in my solid subjects. You can be sure that I will use the ritual every Sunday evening until I finish college!"

Charlie G. has this to report: "After six months of job hunting (as a laid-off aerospace engineer) my knuckles were raw from knocking on doors and I had writer's cramp from filling out applications, but no sign of a job. My unemployment insurance was just a drop in the proverbial bucket, and my savings were just about gone. Desperate is the calmest word I can think of to describe my feelings about the situation. What did I have to lose? When I considered trying the Gnostic Sacrifice Ritual, I decided that just one energy transformer personality was not enough, so I set my ritual up to read this way: 'I lovingly and willingly sacrifice my frustration to Nergal, my poverty to Osiris, my ineffectiveness to Ishtar and my disorganization to Abraxas. I gladly accept your gifts of power, prosperity, effectiveness and organization, and pledge their efficient use in improving all areas of my life. I ask your special help in focusing the energy to bring me a GOOD job right away. Thank you all.' I used the ritual at bedtime, then again the next morning. I planned to use it twice a day until something happened, but this is all it took. I was getting ready for another day of beating the bushes when my phone rang. It was a call for a job—and it turned out to be a better position than the one I lost in the lay-off! Now I know that the energy transformer personalities are my friends. Working with them makes life easier and much more fruitful."

THE GNOSTIC RITUAL OF JOY—YOUR PERMANENT AND POSITIVE CONTACT WITH THE ENERGY TRANSFORMER PERSONALITIES

Obviously we need more than the simple sacrifice ritual to get a thorough working relationship with the energy transformer personalities, and through them the elementals and nature spirits who can be so wonderfully helpful to you also. And nothing could be better for this happy task than the *Gnostic Ritual of Joy*. You will find this the natural and safe way to meet and commune with the basic, primordial forces of the universe; make friends with them; and learn to LET them bring the highest good into all areas of your life. Think of this as a wooing or courtship rite designed in a party atmosphere to bring you the loving good favor of the entities you need to enhance your personal progress and well-being. Thus the preparations for the ritual should be quite like your personal preparations for a special date with the person of your dreams. Make yourself as attractive and pleasant as possible, and set aside a place for the courting that is also as attractive and pleasant as possible. This is an excellent time to indulge in candles and incense if they are at all compatible with your ideas of beauty and luxury, and the use of a good perfume oil or cologne should go without saying. (I personally prefer "power oil" which is a mixture of citron and frankincense.) Other than this, you require no props other than your own mind, feelings and body, and a bit of party type food and drink. For the beverage I suggest your choice of a nice brandy, red wine, orange juice or grape juice. For the food, I prefer almonds for their reputed health-giving qualities and low calories, but candy mints, corn chips or any festive food will do.

The ritual itself should begin with the Gnostic Ritual for Effectiveness, but this time it is best not to write, read and burn the affirmation. You should be familiar enough with it to handle it from memory. Care not a whit about verbal accuracy, but do say in your own words something like this, "I lovingly and willingly offer the sacrifice of my ineffectiveness to Ishtar and my disorganization to Abraxas, and gladly accept your gifts of effectiveness and organization. I pledge their use in uplifting all areas of my life, and invite your help in meeting and enjoying the energy transformer personalities, elementals and nature spirits now. Thank you."

Next, say aloud, "Now, good friends, let's get to the party." Then lift your chalice or glass as if to salute or toast a friend and speak, "Brother Nergal, I toast our friendship and feel the joy of sharing food and drink with you." Then have a nice sip of your drink, put it down, salute Nergal by gesture with a piece of the food and have a bite. When your mouth is again empty and ready for conversation, say, "Now I want to feel closer to you, so I will focus all my attention on you and your special energy." Then hold the palm of one hand about an inch in front of your root center to feel the energy flowing out of it, and make a real effort to think and feel as (or in tune with) the energy transformer source. This will take anywhere from 30 seconds to say ten minutes, depending on how it feels to you. Remember, this is like deepening a friendship at a party; do what you *feel*.

When you feel the closer friendship with Nergal, you are ready to repeat the process with Ra, then with Ishtar, Osiris, Marduk and Thoth in turn. I find it most comfortable to address these first six as "brother," then Bast as "sister," but each will respond well to either salutation—they are not hung up on sexual status or the like, so your personal feelings or preference will be fine. (I'm sure that some scholars will want to use the female salutation to Ishtar, for instance, and the personality will understand and relate to you just as nicely that way.)

Next complete the process for Bast, and you have deepened your relationship and mutual understanding with all seven major psychic centers of your body. Then you are ready to approach the super power of the extra-bodily personalities. Lift your glass in salutation to Mother Isis, and in your communion period with her, feel all the positive qualities of loving motherhood focused on you along with the special receptivity and loyalty. Feel Isis as the purely personal part of

the Godhead, even as you will understand the purely imperso-
nal (yet intensely involved) power of Abraxas. To me there is
not a fitting salutation for the pure principle that is Abraxas,
so I address it as principle by using just the name spoken three
times, "Abraxas, Abraxas, Abraxas, I toast our friendship..,"
and in a strangely abstract way you will find a union with the
principle of all interpersonal relationships.

CONCLUDING THE RITUAL OF JOY

Remember to keep the party spirit going throughout. You
have now paid your respects to and enjoyed the guest of honor,
but we will enjoy mingling now with the many other fun
guests. Lift your glass once more and say, "I toast my friends,
the elementals, all nature spirits, and all who are close to me
in the spirit realms. I invite your touch and caresses along
with your inspiration and guidance. Let's enjoy each other to
the fullest." Then relax and do or say whatever you feel.
Sometimes you will find yourself just sitting peacefully
enjoying a feeling of good fellowship, other times you may be
talking over one or more of your personal problems, or you
may be "hit" with a wonderful new idea. You will find the
ritual different every time you use it, even as each party you
give or attend is different from all the others. When you feel it
is time to go, thank all your friends (individually or collec-
tively as the spirit moves you) and invite them to work and
play in an ever-growing closeness with you.

Notice that we have stressed the party atmosphere and
good fellowship almost to the exclusion of anything resem-
bling a specific request for help. In many ways this is like a
good business cocktail party; you may not ask anyone to sign
a contract or order right then but the stage is set by the
mutuality of the relationship to accomplish great things
together. Then one day shortly after the party, the phone rings
with the order or request to drop by with the contract. This is
the low key form of "salesmanship" that succeeds on the
basis of mutuality where all the pressure in the world would
fail.

How often should you use this ritual? ... How often do you like to go to a party? Some people like it every night; others just once a month or even less. I suggest that you plan a "biggie" for the night of the new moon with others less elaborate along the way according to your own taste. Be a good spirit party giver and you will quickly understand why I can say with complete accuracy about myself and any form of duty or acitvity: "If I can't have a good time, I'm not going— and that includes my own funeral!" You will take your good time with you WHEREVER you go.

POSITIVE BENEFITS FROM THE RITUAL OF JOY

L.W. had this to report on his first use of the ritual of joy: "I'm a day person so I held my first ritual of joy party right after lunch. When I finished and went outside I had a most amazing experience with the cows in the pasture. One cow came over to me as I was looking over the fence, and suddenly I really *felt* a sense of kinship and oneness with all the animals in the field; we were all expressions of the same Light, with basically the same feelings and needs, though in different physical forms. (I knew this intellectually and even emotionally before, but to be able to really perceive it is something else entirely!) Some of these cows were being sent to the butcher in a couple of weeks and I felt that the cow who came to the fence (she let me pet her which wasn't usual for any of them) was asking for a share of the good influence from my ritual work for herself and all the others who were about to leave the physcial plane.

"It was almost as if she were the priestess seeking spirit contact for the 'tribe'—though with me as an intermediary. Naturally I asked Ishtar, Isis and Co. to send blessings and protection to the animals from then on. Somehow the good effects from this carried over the whole farm and into all areas of my life. My sister's dreadfully independent housecat became very affectionate and several times insisted on joining me when I repeated the ritual of joy. And the whole world has changed for me. It no longer seems hostile. I am followed with 'lucky breaks' of all kinds. Yes, my income has more than doubled and all financial worries have faded away, but it is my vibrant health and new energy and the moment-by-moment extra fullness and enjoyment of life that I consider the important part of the results."

H.N. had this to report: "I enjoyed performing the ritual of joy, but it was not until the third day after I did it that I began to feel anything of a really great improvement. That night I was awakened out of a deep sleep and was given a love message on the crystal of my watch. Just as soon as I read it, it faded away and the watch looked 'normal' again. Then I felt that my whole system and beingness had been cleansed of all negativity and ineffectiveness.

"The next day I really never felt so good. You can believe that the more positive attitude and frame of mind was quite welcome. My husband, who had been virtually ignoring me and seriously talking about divorce, suddenly became especially loving and attentive. Something happened to add a whole new dimension to our sex life, and he comes home to me every night; he hasn't had a 'night out with the boys' since this started, and we have launched a program of learning to be ever more satisfying sex partners for each other.

"Within six weeks my husband got a promotion and raise on his job and I got a very nice raise with many compliments on my good work on my own job. Than I got up the nerve to tell my husband about the ritual of joy and we did it together. Words will never describe the difference in our whole lives. All the little problems and irritations just seemed to fade away. A couple of apparently sour investments suddenly perked up and more than doubled our money where we had expected a big loss. Now our savings and investment programs are in such good shape that we could retire right now, but we're having so much fun working that we agreed to keep at it for several more years, then take a six-month round the world trip to launch our retirement. It's a rich, full life now, where before I was on the verge of utter despair. Tell all your students to TRY IT—I guarantee they will be enriched beyond anything they dare hope for."

D.C. sent us this bit of happy news: "The most wonderful thing happened to me after I performed the ritual of joy! As you know I had been planning to get married, but my daughter was violently opposed to it until two days after the ritual. That evening she wanted to know why I was not with my man and I explained that I did not want to leave her alone, and besides I wanted to rest. She insisted that I get dressed and go to him. I was speechless for I had been very up-tight about this problem. I was waiting for the right moment to tell her our plans but couldn't figure out how to or when. Quickly the wedding plans were made, and now we are a wonderfully happy family. One interesting side note—with all the pressure and resentment from my daughter and my natural lack of snoopiness, it was rather pleasant to discover that my new husband is quite substantially wealthy. I had lived at a near poverty level for more years than I care to remember, but now we live in the lap of luxury. Life is wonderful."

HOW TO TAILOR THE GNOSTIC RITUAL OF JOY FOR MAXIMUM EFFECTIVENESS IN <u>YOUR</u> LIFE

The first time I used the ritual of joy the party seemed a little flat. True, I got some very nice results, but I instinctively knew that it should be much better. We are all very different in our ideas of what makes a really special party, and it is here that your individuality can become your most important asset. Most of you will feel a bit sloppy or flat at your first production of the ritual of joy, but you were not an expert the first time you tried anything else in the life either! This is like the point in a computer programming course where we get the opportunity to put the theory into practice—think of it as your first "hands on the equipment" session. If the computer didn't roll over and bark for you on your first command, you certainly didn't decide that computers are no good, or even that you can't program them. Instead you took a good look at your process to see where you goofed. In my own first ritual of joy, fun-loving and joker type though I am, I was still a bit too up-tight about it—but then remember back to the *first* time YOU gave a party for a bunch of really special people.

I've tried to give you a feel for the approach. Think of your first two or three performances of the ritual of joy as practice sessions—say you were so interested in the success of your party that you tried a few dry runs using dummies or manikins to simulate the guests. You don't really expect a lot of response from a manikin, so you relax about that part and focus on ideas for making your party more fun for the guests. Again, here is where your individual tastes come in. At some "grown up" parties, you may find the guests playing "kid" games like *Pin the Tail on the Donkey* or even *Monopoly* and having a ball at it. At the other extreme you may give something like an old Roman orgy—or anything in between. YOU are indeed the life of this party, so plan it for the kind of FUN that appeals to you right at the time of the ritual. Then RELAX and really enter into the spirit of the thing—and I can guarantee that your party will be a smashing success.

The keynote here is to relax, be yourself and have a ball. Give your party for the sheer joy of the party itself, not asking for special or immediate favors, but simply sharing a new level of oneness with the whole of the unseen side of life. And practice! Keep giving the parties until you have all the bugs out of YOU, and really enjoy them. And I promise you that every time you use the ritual of joy, no matter how sloppily, there will be some form of a thank-you from your spirit friends that will indeed manifest into your material life within a week or less. Keep trying it—not till you get it right, but till you make it really FUN. There is not a better or nicer way to uplift your whole life. Please stop and perform the ritual of joy at least once before you go on to the next chapter.

GNOSTIC MAGIC MIND JOGGERS

1. Study the table that gives you an overview of the GNOS-TIC MAGIC POWER STRUCTURE to get a good feel for the completeness and total effectiveness of the powers you will be using.

2. The energy transformer personalities bear the names of ancient magical deities; think of them in either (or both) way that is comfortable to you, but get the understanding of the area of your life that can be enhanced by each.
3. You can use the modified ritual of sacrifice to gain immediate help and solutions to pressing problems. Don't hesitate to try; it can only help. Use it and win!
4. The Gnostic Ritual of Joy will put you in permanent and positive contact with the power and help of the energy transformer personalities, the elementals and nature spirits, and your own personal spirit helpers.
5. The Gnostic Ritual of Joy is a loving PARTY—use it in a party mood and you will find sweeping and wonderful changes in all areas of your life.
6. Your own individuality is the most important ingredient of the ritual of joy. Tailor it to be the most fun for you, and the response from the unseen world will be maximized and magnificent.
7. Relax and USE the ritual of joy; there will be positive benefits every time you do. Please use the ritual at least once before you go on to the work of the next chapter.

3

Build Your Gnosis of Oneness, Protection and Power Now

The feeling of good fellowship and shared fun that you developed in the Gnostic Ritual of Joy in our last chapter sets the foundation for your oneness, protection, power and all the rest of the work of this book. I urge you to practice it in joy as often as you find time, until you regularly feel the company of your unseen but very real friends throughout your normal routine of living. Remember that we spoke of the Gnosis first as a *knowing*, and it is the knowing that you are never alone that counts here. At first you may feel slightly silly or that you are kidding yourself—this is the normal put-down from the intellect or front mind—but just a few sessions will see a budding reality that will quickly grow into a fullness of joy and companionship. Bring your unseen friends along to join you now in the ABRAXAS RITUAL OF ONENESS AND PROTECTION.

A DEEPER LOOK AT THE CONCEPT OF A GNOSIS

To you as a practical Gnostic Magician, the idea of a Gnosis is much more than a simple knowing—it is a living reality, so strong and complete that it has a separate and virtually permanent life of its own. When thinking of protection, for instance, most of you will remember an old toothpaste commercial on TV where a baseball was prevented from reaching the target it was thrown at by an "invisible" wall. Our approach in building your Gnosis of Oneness and Protection is to create a shield that is just as impervious to anything that would affect you negatively as was the glass wall on TV, but to pass the good through to you as if the shield did not exist at all. Similarly, the Gnosis of Prosperity and Riches that you will build later is to be a slot machine that brings you a big jackpot every time you play, and your Gnosis of Perfect Health is a combination of a dynamo of energy and complete immunization against all forms of disease. This solid a reality is naturally not built in an instant. Rather we might think of it as knitting a sweater or a sock; it is done one stitch or one row at a time. The completed product may take a few days or even a few weeks in process, but the end result is certainly worth much more than the effort you put into it, particularly because every step of the way will be full of fun.

Since a Gnosis of Oneness with the Infinite is a major factor in all of our more advanced work, we will illustrate the process by working together to build yours, with the happy fallout of a Gnosis of Perfect Protection as part of the natural process.

PREPARATION TO BUILD YOUR GNOSIS OF ONENESS AND PROTECTION

Metaphysicians of all ages have told us of our natural oneness with the Infinite, and mystics regale us with poetic accounts of their personal experience of the feeling. But all of this is talk, with no practical value to YOU until it ceases to be an intellectual exercise and becomes a living Gnosis. Yet we have to start somewhere, and the simplest form of preparation begins with a brief look at the nature of oneness.

The illusion of separateness is created by the visible part of the material world. You see physical boundaries to your body and so accept it when you are told by the establishment that you are an individual, an island, completely separate from all other beings. But the visible part of the material world provides you with far less than 10% of your total mental/emotional experience or inputs. And while it is quite true that your material body has distinct finite boundaries, you also have finer bodies, each of which blends more completely into perfect oneness, as in the preachings of the mystics. As we unfold the work of this book, we will resolve the paradox of perfect individuality and total oneness for you and let you prove to yourself that each principle is totally true and not at all contradictory—but this will grow on you as you contemplate the magnificence of the RESULTS you will be getting from your Gnostic Magic.

Our purpose here is to remove the barriers to oneness for you on the mental/emotional level so that you will have the power to build your Gnosis of Perfect Protection out of the raw material of living oneness. Join me in remembering that the *life force* which powers your body is the same force that powers mine—and that powers the life of the goat, the cow, the fern, grain or even the amoeba! We are all traveling on spaceship earth, sharing its life support systems and indeed deriving even the substance for our physical bodies from each other. Our modern economic system illustrates more fully the complete interdependence of individuals upon each other. Do you know ANYONE who makes or produces everything he eats, drinks, wears and uses? Of course not! There is also deeper evidence of oneness when we dig beneath the purely material level to consider emotional and mental relationships. It would be easy for you to contemplate these self-evident truths and experience a mystic's *oneness with all that is*, except for your negative emotions. The resentments and prejudices you have built or accepted make you want to exclude certain people (or, in this ending quarter of the 20th century, even whole races or ethnic groups), but to exclude one being from the oneness is to quite effectively exclude yourself.

Thus the preparation for building your Gnosis of Oneness and Protection is a frontal assault on your prejudices, resentments and lurking hatreds. True, you may have been grievously wronged by another human being, so much so that you are totally justified in hating that person. But the price of harboring such a negative emotion is greater than you can afford to pay. Aside from the toxins and poisons released into your system by feelings of hatred and resentment, you just cannot afford to cut yourself off from the Infinite and try to make a happy life ON YOUR OWN. The trick here is to make a list of all your former or present antagonists or "enemies," and begin one at a time to pray for their spiritual growth AND for their financial and material well-being.

If you feel yourself holding back on one or more of these people, do a careful sacrifice ritual—sacrifice your frustration to Nergal, your resentment (and/or hatred) to Ra, and your separateness to Ishtar. Repeat the sacrifice ritual (using the written form as we learned it in our opening chapters) until you KNOW that you have made your psychic and emotional peace with each person on your list. When this is completed, you are ready to build your Gnosis of Oneness and Protection.

Here I will pause to tease you, as I teased the members of my experimental class at E.S.P. Lab where the groundwork for this book was firmly laid: In a few weeks when you come to me to complain that some part of the magic is not working for you, I'll catch you on this step; the MAJOR cause of all your magical blanks or misfires is a chink in your armor of oneness caused by not fully completing this step of the preparation.

BENEFITS FROM THE PROCESS OF PREPARATION FOR THE ONENESS AND PROTECTION RITUAL

Jessie G. had a terrible conflict with her supervisor and was constantly in fear of being fired. She felt harassed all the time on her job and wanted to quit, but at 60 she was afraid she would never find a suitable new job. Let's let her continue:

"When you spoke of the preparation for the ritual of oneness and protection, I felt that I would have to give up this form of magical work. The conflict with Clara, my boss, seemed far too great an obstacle to ever turn loose of just to find that abstraction you called oneness. But I thought it over and decided I had very little to lose by trying. I wrote my sacrifice affirmation, 'I lovingly and willingly sacrifice my frustration to Nergal, my resentment of Clara to Ra, and my feelings of separateness to Ishtar. I gladly accept your gifts of fulfillment, peace and oneness, and pledge their efficient application to improve all areas of my life. Please help me. Thank you.' I started this on a Friday night after a really miserable week on the job. It was hard on Friday but I knew that I had two more days before going back to that hellhole of an office. Saturday went a little better, and Sunday night, after I finished the sacrifice ritual, I could and did actually pray for Clara's spiritual growth and material success. Somehow, my aura must have beaten me to the office on Monday morning. Clara greeted me with a smile, which I warmly returned. She called me into her office and said she felt we had been having an unnecessary conflict. She asked me to try to work with her in peace and friendship and simply forget our problems of the past. I agreed very willingly. Now it is three months later— and you wouldn't believe the difference. Clara and I are fast friends, the job is a joy, I know I'm doing much better work, and this was just recognized in the most tangible manner—a MERIT RAISE with Clara's approval! The fact that this cleared the way for my later magic seems almost beside the point; this one little sacrifice ritual turned my life from misery to enjoyment all by itself!"

When G.T. heard about the preparation for the oneness ritual, her eyes flashed fire as she blurted, "How do you expect me to forgive the bitch who just seduced my husband?" Again it was my turn to ask, "Do you prefer to let her destroy your whole life by cutting you off from your source of power, life and protection?" G.T. sputtered a moment and then grudgingly agreed to try the sacrifice ritual. Here is her report: "I had some reservations about the sacrifice of my hatred of E., but you convinced me it was necessary to try. I used the written affirmation, and it took several days before I felt my release. All at once I felt clean inside. I saw how clearly I had contributed to the situation with my husband, and realized that we had already talked it out and started a new life together. Than I saw how my harbored resentment was sowing the seeds for later problems, and I was GLAD to be *free* from the negative feelings. Of course the oneness ritual came easy for me after this, but also there is a fresh and lovely relationship with my husband. I realize that for months, *I* had kept the other woman between us, long after he had given her up. It's a happy and wonderful life now—thanks to you and those wonderful energy transformer personalities!"

HOW TO PERFORM THE GNOSTIC RITUAL OF ONENESS AND PROTECTION

For any important ritual, I like to set the mood with candles, incense, and power oil; but this is a matter of personal taste, the important thing being only the setting of a mood of oneness and *joy*. Prepare as for the basic sacrifice ritual, with a written affirmation and place to drop the burning paper. For this ritual the affirmation of sacrifice and benefit should be written this way: "I lovingly and willingly sacrifice my frustration to Nergal, all of my remaining resentments to Ra, my separateness to Ishtar and my defenselessness to Abraxas. I happily accept your gifts of fulfillment, peace, oneness and perfect protection; and ask your help in moulding them into my living Gnosis of Oneness and Protection. I feel it forming and taking a life of its own to live with me forevermore, making my life an example of oneness and protection for all to see. My loving thanks."

When the mood is set, sit at your work space (or altar as I prefer to call it), picture yourself bathed in loving white Light, and begin to read the affirmation. Read the affirmation with *feeling*, really entering into the spirit of the sacrifice ritual, three times. On the fourth time, touch the upper left-hand corner of the paper to the candle flame, then read the affirmation again, slightly ahead of the flame, and drop the residue gently into the place you prepared for it. Then sit quietly and enjoy the feeling of the growth of your Gnosis of

Oneness and Protection. At least it should be a very pleasant few moments, and for many it will include a very special set of feelings and experiences.

Apparent results may vary widely, both at the time of the ritual and afterwards, but they are always positive. You will be able to tell from the way things feel to you whether you should repeat the ritual several times over a period of a few days or whether it "took" the first time. And I suggest that it should be renewed roughly once a month for the rest of your life—but that, too, is a matter of your taste and feeling.

Ted D. had this to report on his ritual. "Al, you know me as a hardheaded business man, but that Gnostic Ritual of Oneness and Protection really brought out the mystic in me. I used the affirmation exactly as it was given to me, and on the fourth time, as I dropped the paper into the waiting ashtray, I had a most magnificent mystic experience. It was as if there were no boundaries even to my physical body—I could feel the life in the tree outside my window and a special comrade-ship with the fly still buzzing in my room. Somehow I felt the words of the 91st Psalm, 'A thousand will fall at your side and ten thousand at your right hand, but it will not come near you. ... Because he clings fast to me in love, I will deliver him. I will set him free and honor him. With long life will I satisfy him, and show him my salvation,' spoken not as the words of a poet, but AS THE LAW OF THE UNIVERSE in relation to ME! As to down-to-earth results—how can I put it, it may be a matter of attitude, but my business has never been better and it promises to be really magnificent; I feel I'm in perfect health with lots of extra vitality; my marriage is happy and satisfying and I feel that I am growing spiritually as well as materially. It is generally wonderful—I might have said too good to be true, but in the oneness I KNOW that I am worthy of it."

Alice Y. reported: "I performed the Gnostic Oneness and Protection ritual exactly as it was given to me. At the time, I didn't feel much of anything, but I repeated it for three consecutive evenings. I do feel better about my relationship to the universe now, but the tangible things are what really prove the value of the ritual. A series of long-standing irritating problems seemed to solve themselves in a most satisfying manner. Then I got a promotion and a better than 30% raise in salary! And I met a most wonderful man—it was sort of a whirlwind courtship and we plan to be married next month. All this happened within three weeks of my performing the ritual. You can be sure that I will follow your suggestion of renewing it once a month!"

PREPARING TO BUILD YOUR GNOSIS OF POWER

The real preparation for building your Gnosis of Power is the successful completion of the ritual of joy and the oneness and protection ritual. With these working for you, you KNOW that you are always surrounded by friendly helpers in the unseen world, and that in the oneness you are not only completely protected, but you fully realize your worthiness for good and growth. In this feeling of joyously fitting well into your universe, you will recognize the truth in the statement that *mastery of your fate is your birthright*. Even as you feel that your perfect protection is a law of the universe, so you will feel that your personal power to be and do and to achieve is also a universal law.

Your Gnosis of Oneness and Protection may seem to be primarily on the feeling level, and that is good because it is from there that it is effective. But we want to add a fresh degree of tangibility for your Gnosis of Power. We will prepare by creating a mental picture which you will bring to life in the Gnostic Power Ritual. First imagine a huge electric generator or dynamo floating above your head. See it connected by strong power lines to each of your seven chakras or psychic centers. Make your dynamo big enough so it is easy to feel that in your normal routine of living you are using far less than ½% of its power output. Next, imagine a cable connecting the dynamo to a large computer which is programmed to control its power output. Then picture a computer terminal running to the energy transformer personality concerned with each of your seven chakras, and a corresponding monitor line from your chakras to the terminals monitored by the energy transformer personalities. If this picture seems too complicated, take any one or two of the three major parts and you will be able to get the same excellent results. The key here is to build a clear mental picture that is both comfortable and deeply meaningful to you. Then we will bring it to life in the Gnostic Power Ritual.

BUILDING YOUR GNOSIS OF POWER WITH THE GNOSTIC POWER RITUAL

To complete the preparation, write a fresh ritual of sacrifice affirmation that you may consider the "granddaddy of them all." It should read like this: "I lovingly and willingly sacrifice my frustration to Nergal, my resentments to Ra, my ineffectiveness to Ishtar, my weakness to Osiris, my barrenness to Marduk, my confusion to Toth, my attachment to Bast, my unreceptivity to Isis and my disorganization to Abraxas. I gladly accept your gifts of fulfillment, Light, effectiveness, strength, creativity, awareness, unattachment, receptivity and organization, and invite your help in applying these great forces to the building of my Gnosis of Power. I feel all of this magnificent energy flowing into my mental picture of the dynamo and computer and the wonderful energy transformer personalities monitoring my needs and progress, and I feel it being born into living reality now. I pledge its efficient use to make all areas of my life better and to enhance my personal growth. Thank you all for this wonderful help."

It is well to precede this ritual with the Ritual of Joy to be sure that the mood is just right. But if you feel very good and at one with the universe, you may start it with the simple mood setting of candles and incense and picturing yourself in the Light. When you are ready, first rebuild the mental picture of the dynamo, computer, and terminals being monitored by your friends in joy. Then read the sacrifice affirmation with feeling and spirit three times, and on the fourth, touch the upper left-hand corner of the paper to your candle as before and read it just ahead of the flame. As you drop the paper into the prepared container, try to visualize the life-force fully entering your mental image, and FEEL the system being switched "on" to insure your personal auric power and *power to achieve* forever more.

Repeat the ritual for at least three consecutive days (or evenings), and each time feel a greater reality in your mental pictures. Keep it up until you KNOW that you can mentally or aloud call on the name of an energy transformer personality and get an instant flow of tremendous extra energy through his or her chakra.

APPLYING YOUR GNOSIS OF POWER TO ACHIEVE YOUR MOST CHERISHED GOALS

Earlier in this chapter we commented that less than 10% of your total inputs are from strictly physical (five sense) sources. Now let's recognize that you have something over 90% of any other person's inputs to influence by means of your Gnosis of Power. Thus you can broadcast your sense of power and personal worth to the world and EXPECT it to respond by giving you the full respect and cooperation that you so naturally deserve in striving toward your well-chosen goals. Those of you who have worked with my *Magic of New Ishtar Power* will recognize that the whole book was basically devoted to THE POWER TO ACHIEVE. But now, with the proper execution of the Gnostic Ritual of Power, you have built a system of even greater effectiveness! The world awaits your calculated application of this power to shower you with success and riches beyond the limits of your imagination.

In all our earlier work, the POWER TO ACHIEVE was left to the discretion of Ishtar and the other energy trans-former personalities, but now you are taking the next step toward your complete MASTERSHIP by entering fully and consciously into the process. In our class, one of my students likened this to being able to slip your system into "passing gear" to bring in the extra power to literally overwhelm the auras of your would-be adversaries and make them your willing associates. If the "passing gear" idea appeals to you, use it, but regardless of the concept, do develop the willingness to call on one or more of the energy transformer personalities for a big shot of energy as you go into any sort of work or discussion.

As usual, the easiest way to illustrate this application is to share the reports of those who have used it successfully already. One very typical type of report came from Gene U.: "My company, at least in jobs like mine, has an unstated policy of simply letting your work pile up on your desk while you're away on vacation. On the last day of my two-week vacation I got to contemplating the mound of work that would be waiting for me with more than a little dread. I had been working with the preliminary stages of Gnostic Magic, so this seemed like an ideal time to work on my Gnosis of Power, with the special idea of polishing off the huge mound of work I knew would be waiting for me in the morning. As I went through the ritual I mentally asked for help at work in the morning. Sure enough when I got to the office, there was an even bigger pile of waiting tasks than I had expected. But I decided to be undaunted and give the Gnosis a chance—it was a beautiful idea! Normally when I get back from a two-week vacation, it takes three or four weeks of hard work to get caught up. This time with an even bigger accumulation, I was right up to snuff in just three and a half days! There's no way to tell you how wonderful it feels to catch up so effortlessly! In fact, the big boss noticed it, too, and told me that I am now next in line for a promotion."

D.K.'s report was a bit more colorful, but it expresses the sentiments of many who have used the ritual well: "I have come to think of the Gnosis of Power Ritual as sort of a combination of the phone booth where Clark Kent changes into Superman and the can of spinach for Popeye! I can never make a suitable list of the accomplishments the Power to Achieve that comes from the ritual has brought me, but here are a few happy highlights: I was right on the brink of having my mortgage forclosed with the consequent loss of my house, when the power opened the way to a magnificent bit of impossible refinancing, so I kept the house and got lower payments and even a reduced interest rate to boot! I was at rock bottom when I started this work—I needed money, love, health, opportunity and a long series of lucky breaks; and Ishtar's power to achieve and the Gnostic Power Ritual came through every time, with time and money to spare. My income has more than tripled, I feel happy, healthy, admired, loved, lucky and full of hope and opportunity for the future. It's a happy life now, no longer full of despair, but full of zest and the knowledge that far more than one 'somebody up there' likes me and watches over me. Thanks to all who have had a part in introducing me to this great power!"

HINTS ON FOCUSING AND TROUBLE-SHOOTING YOUR MAGICAL POWER TO MAXIMIZE YOUR RESULTS

By this point in the work, YOU should have already generated some powerfully positive results, quite like the feedback reports I have shared with you. If you are not ecstatically happy with your progress, pause to look at the load of excess baggage you are carrying—not only does it hold you back, but it saps your strength as well. Here is a brief list of the hangers-on who will delight in holding back your progress and keeping you a slave to their own negative ways. Think of them as very unsavory people to be avoided for the sake of simple cleanliness, as well as for your physical and psychological good health. I call them "Danny Despair," "Pete the Pessimist," "Nora the Nag," "Sammy the Shirker," and "Sharky the Cynic." They like you to play their roles for them, and delight in the mess it makes out of your life. Avoid acting like any of these nasty people as if your happy life depended on it—because IT DOES!

But note carefully that our list does not include the role of the skeptic. Indeed, *open-minded* skepticism is just about the safest and most intelligent approach to any part of the occult. And it should help you keep your good humor. The attitude of "I'm really not sure about this, but I'll try it just for fun," will keep you out of trouble and help you prove the wonderful practicality of these principles faster than any other approach I might suggest. Good Gnostic Magic does not require blind faith; you're far too intelligent for that approach—it became obsolete with mass public education. Substitute the good-natured and good-humored experimental mood and let your RESULTS prove the working reality of all that we are striving to teach you.

With all of this in mind, let's set up a check list for your effective use of this much of our Gnostic Magical program:

1. Are you working to avoid and eliminate any and all of the negative roles of despair, pessimism, nagging, shirking or cynicism?
2. Are you enjoying every moment of your ritual work?
3. Do you still feel the friendly presences from your Gnostic Ritual of Joy? If not, repeat it as soon as possible, and before you try the more advanced work.
4. Do you FEEL the oneness with all creation and the loving protection of the Infinite that comes with it? If not, take a good look at the need for more sacrifice of your resentments and old hatreds. Then redo the ritual of oneness and protection and make it a living reality in your daily life.
5. When you can give an enthusiastic YES to all of these, your Gnostic Power Ritual will indeed bring you the power to achieve your most cherished goals. Strive on and WIN!

D.Z. gave us a typical report on the trouble-shooting: "I felt like the whole world was against me, and the Gnostic Magic was my last hope. But when I used the rituals, nothing happened. I was really playing the role of Danny Despair. When I finally tried your check list, I had to answer 'no' to all four questions. At least that told me where my effort should go. I decided to clean up my act and try again on the fun level instead of with all the tension I had obviously used before. This time the ritual of joy really was one, and the feeling carried over very well into the oneness ritual. And my first application of the Gnostic Power Ritual (after the clean-up) produced positive results! They were little things like $100 more on my income tax refund than I expected, being invited to a party by the same people who had snubbed me about a similar party three months ago, then a raise in pay *twice* what I had expected. As you said, now I have a handle on it and I KNOW that I will be a happily successful Gnostic Magician.''

GNOSTIC MAGIC MIND JOGGERS

1. A Gnosis is much more than a simple knowing. It is a living reality, so vital and complete that it has a separate and virtually permanent life of its own.
2. Prepare to build your Gnosis of Oneness and Protection with the two key steps:
   A. Recognize that the illusion of separateness is part of the material world, but in the unseen world oneness can be and is a total reality.
   B. Remove the barriers to your oneness arising from negative feelings about other people; use the special sacrifice ritual to give up your hatred and resentments.
3. The benefits from the preparation for the ritual of oneness are magnificent in themselves and give you a nice extra set of rewards for your trouble.
4. Take the feeling of your ritual of joy with you into the performance of the Gnostic Ritual of Oneness and Protection, and make it the law of the universe to you.
5. Mastery of your fate is your birthright. Successful completion of the ritual of joy and the oneness and protection rituals make you ready for your Gnosis of Power. Build the mental images and take them to your work space to complete your Gnosis of Power and fill yourself with the power to achieve your most cherished goals.
6. Be sure to apply your new power quickly; test it and prove its great value to you.
7. If you feel that your progress is not wonderful, go to the check list and work to change all your *no* answers to the enthusiastic *yes.* Then redo your Gnostic Power Ritual and join the ranks of the big winners!

4

Million-Dollar Magic Gnosis for Money, Jewels, Automobiles—Anything You Desire!

In all your life and all your travels, have you ever met a person who complained of having too much money? If so, you've met one of the earth's really rare creatures! For the vast majority of people, earning or otherwise ethically acquiring more money is high on their list of goals. If this is not true of you, you may do well to skip this chapter for now and plan to come back to it for background later. For the rest, let's have a go at harnessing the good Gnostic Magic for a big boost in your income and accumulated personal fortune.

GETTING BETTER ACQUAINTED WITH MONEY AND RICHES

In order to work effectively with or for money, it's a good idea to be sure we know enough about it. We will have a look at the size and scope, color and texture, taste and feel, and number and rhythm of money now, just as we will take that close a look at love/friendship and health in our upcoming chapters.

Far too many people have lurking or subliminally negative ideas about money, arising mostly from brainwashing

during childhood. Were you taught, "Blessed are the poor...,"
or "Love of money is the root of all evil?" The "blessed are the
poor" thing was an Oriental way of indicating the value of
modesty and had nothing to do with poverty, but it is often
misconstrued to tell you that poverty is a virtue, so riches
must be a vice. The second one should say LACK of money is
the root of most evil! The ancient Vedantic concepts of Prana
may help our understanding here; Prana is the energy of
sustenance of all beings, thus is the life force itself, and it is
recognized or symbolized on the material level simply as
money. Thus we could say on solid Vedantic grounds that
money is a symbolic claim to more life, and it correlates
perfectly with the New Testament statement, "I am come
that they might have life, and that more abundantly."

It should be easy to get comfortable with the basic size
and scope of money from that standpoint, but how about your
feelings when you see a magnificent yacht, or a big chauffeur-
driven limousine with all the perquisites? The slightest tinge
of jealousy is an indication that you have more work to do in
your relationship to riches. The proper feeling here was well
put to me when I was a Department of Defense Auditor at
work on a government contract. The firm in question main-
tained a very expensive dining room for the exclusive use of
its top ten executives and their guests—of course all at
company expense, and I teased the young, low-paid junior
accountant whom the company had assigned to me for
liaison, "Doesn't that fancy dining room make you jealous?"
His answer was right to our point; he said, "Not at all. One of
these days I'm going to be in there, too, and I like it just the
way it is." Happiness *inside* when you see super success and
even ostentation for others is the prerequisite to the building
of your Gnosis of Money and Riches. Take a good look at your
feelings and be prepared to sacrifice all your envy, jealousy and
feelings of unfairness about the distribution of money. You
will recognize this as the first step in your preparation to be
rich and prosperous.

PREPARING TO BUILD YOUR GNOSIS TO MANIFEST MONEY AND RICHES

Once you are rid of your negative feelings and hang-ups about money, it's a good idea to spend a few minutes wallowing in the pleasantness of contemplated riches. Think about the taste and feel, and the color and texture of money. Remember that abundant money caters to your taste because it will buy you the luxuries and perquisites of financial rank—think of how nice that will feel, and feel it as if it were so NOW.

As to texture, picture a nice combination of pretty piles of large-denomination bills and many extra numbers in your checking and savings accounts, and revel in it. Then think back to the mystical and occult beginnings of our country and its monetary system. Remember the pyramid and all-seeing eye on the back of your dollar bill, and know that it is no accident that the color of our paper money is *green*. This is the color of your earthy, Osiris-ruled heart center. Now recall the heart center part of your ritual of joy as you *think* and *feel* Osiris green. Let the earthy qualities of Osiris fill you with the strength and drive on the material level to manifest lots of solid green.

Next consider the number and rhythm of money—the number is 8, which connotes organization and big business. And the rhythm of money beats magically everywhere. There is certainly a rhythm to receiving money; it may be a weekly or monthly paycheck, quarterly dividends on your stocks or savings accounts, your author's semi-annual royalty checks, or an annual thing like the big season of a tax return preparer—but there is a rhythm which correlates with other cycles in the natural and business world. Even the number 8 itself can be logically related to the eight cycle-per-second alpha brain wave (rhythm) which you will find is quite conducive to producing fresh ideas and approaches to business problems.

As we enter this part of the work, we will add extra elements of power, particularly from the energy of number and rhythm. So plan to perform the ritual for manifesting money and riches every day for eight straight days—or better still, plan eight sessions (one a day) followed by eight days off (or working on other things), then eight more sessions, etc., for a total of eight eight-day sessions with eight days off between each group of sessions. Of course you will expect results from the very beginning, but the cumulative effect of the rhythm of eight will bring you ever better results.

HOW TO BUILD YOUR GNOSIS OF RICHES WITH THE GNOSTIC MONEY MANIFESTING RITUAL

As always, set the mood in your work space with your favorite candles and incense, and anoint your brow and heart centers with your favorite prosperity oil (frankincense oil will do very well if you don't already have a favorite). Then, in your own handwriting, write the Gnostic Money Manifesting Chant on a clean piece of paper: "I lovingly and willingly sacrifice my negative feelings about money to Bast, my envy and jealousy of others' riches to Isis, my own lack of riches to Osiris, my ineffectiveness to Ishtar and my disorganization to Abraxas. I gladly accept your gifts of peace, enlightenment, prosperity, effectiveness and organization and pledge their efficient use to vastly improve my financial condition. Please help me to manifest great quantities of money and riches now. My loving thanks to all." (Sign your name exactly as your signature would appear on a check.)

Now hold the piece of paper between the palms of your hands in a comfortable position in front of you (perhaps just as you were taught to hold your hands to pray when you were a little child). Picture yourself bathed in a shaft of bright white Light for a few moments, then speak aloud: "Sister Bast, Mother Isis, Mighty Osiris, Brother Ishtar, Magnificent Abraxas, we have shared joy and sustenance together and it is in that same spirit of good fellowship and joy that I invite your special help now."

Then with plenty of feeling, read your Gnostic Money Manifesting Chant aloud seven times, taking care to sense that you are really giving up the negative feelings and conditions. Then touch the upper edge of the paper to your candle flame and read the chant again just ahead of the flame. As you finish, drop the burning paper into the receptacle you have prepared for it, then relax and sit in silence as long as you enjoy doing so. Let your thoughts drift back to the ideas of savoring the joy of your coming riches, but be sure that everything you think or feel is highly positive and happy. To feel pressure to meet a bill at this point would destroy the power you have worked to build. Be happy. Then when you feel it is finished, thank your friends, snuff out your candles and go back to your normal routine.

As we have suggested before, you may get some very special inspiration or prophetic inputs during the quiet time at the end of your ritual, but don't set up an anxiety situation by expecting it. It is the final scoreboard that counts, so relax and enjoy and know that your help is with you every moment and that your riches are tumbling happily toward you from the beginning of your first chant onward.

BENEFITS FROM THE GNOSTIC MONEY MANIFESTING RITUAL

I regularly get many quickie feedback notes and letters from people who use the ritual for the very first time. Let's begin with this one from J.Y.: "When I finished my first performance of the Gnostic Money Manifesting Ritual, I was completely astonished. I had an urge to count the money in my 'emergency cash envelope' which I keep in my desk. I usually keep fifty dollars there in case something comes up in the middle of the night. Sure enough there was my normal fifty dollars PLUS an extra hundred! I have no idea how it got there, but you can be sure I marched myself right back to my altar and said a big extra thank-you to Bast, Isis, Osiris, Ishtar and Abraxas."

Another typical fast result was reported by M.D.: "I decided that the only time I had to do the Gnostic Money Manifesting Ritual was early in the morning before the rest of the household got up. I did it the first morning, then the second morning. And that SECOND afternoon I got a letter in the mail from Internal Revenue Service. It said I had made a mathematical error on my last year's tax return and enclosed a check for the $312 they said I had overpaid. I didn't bother to check their calculations, but I sure said an enthusiastic thank-you to my nice friends as the start of my next morning's money ritual!"

H.I. had it working this way: "No groceries and only a $5 bill to my name. I went to play Bingo after doing my Gnostic Money Manifesting Ritual and won $450! Thanks to all."

N.T. used the ritual just before leaving for Las Vegas. Here is her report: "The first place I walked into I found three one-dollar bills on the floor. Then 15 minutes later, still playing on their money, I hit a $125 jackpot on the nickel slot machine. Sure was a big help."

But the longer-lasting results are what we want to focus on, just accepting the windfalls and gifts as happy extras. This report from M.H. is really much more in point: "I used the Gnostic Money Manifesting Ritual. For the first eight-day period nothing happened. I waited the next eight days as instructed, then began the ritual again. On the morning of the third day of the second series the owner of the company offered me the position of plant manager at a salary of $30,000 per year. This is a $10,000 raise! Also I'm to be given a few shares of stock in the company and an option to buy more later. I've been with the company for 15 years. Now *this* is progress!"

Another typically nice report was from B.C.: "My birth-day and wedding anniversary were October twelfth, so we decided to go down to Jackpot, Nevada for a few days. I saved and scrimped quite a while to make the trip. I did my money manifesting ritual, gave my Ishtar Medal an extra ceremonial charge, folded my newsletter with the Ishtar paragraph turned outward, and stuck it in my bosom close to my heart. And with much confidence I played Keno. I didn't win just one big one, but *two* of them! I was the first person in the town's history to win twice on one set of numbers! Wow! What a birthday present!"

GNOSTIC MONEY MANAGEMENT—HOW TO PRODUCE AN EVER-GROWING SURPLUS OF RICHES

Many people share a very common complaint, "It's easy to make money, but quite another problem to hang on to some of it!" Emergencies, poor investments, stupid purchases and hand-outs to "friends in need" all too often work together to keep a person or family living from hand to mouth instead of accumulating sizable amounts of money for savings and sound investments. I often tease my students that if they had a savings account with the money from just their last ten years worth of stupid mistakes, it would exceed their annual income—and this statement is virtually never wrong! Obviously having enough self-confidence and discipline to say a firm but pleasant NO at the right time will be a major factor in making you a person of financial means and substance. Let's work on that part first.

The game is literally one of psychological one-upmanship. The friend's ploy is this: "I need your money; you have it; you will feel guilty and miserable if you refuse me." Learn to recognize this one and feel good as you refuse, because giving in would further weaken your friend and certainly deplete your resources. Yes, it's nice to be charitable, but NEVER under psychological pressure.

Similarly the salesman appeals to your ego: "You've worked hard in this world; you're surely worth the price of this bauble." Here the proper response is: "Yes, *I'm worth it*; the question to be answered is, is your product worthy of me?" Similarly, the "con artist" will appeal to your sense of greed with a sure-fire scheme to double or even triple your money in a very short period. If it looks too good to be true, it probably is. And if it's THAT good, why does the person need YOUR money? The rule of thumb here is beware of people offering you a financial favor. There is plenty of money to be made, but it never works for you when it is way outside your own areas of expertise.

Read this section carefully and try to relate it to each of your glaring past mistakes, not for the purpose of beating yourself, but strictly to learn the validity of the statements. Then pass a strict financial rule for yourself: WHEN IN DOUBT OR UNDER PRESSURE, THE ANSWER IS ALWAYS NO. If there is a really good deal for you, it will still be there after you've had time to thoroughly check it out.

As you reflect on your past mistakes, be prepared to sacrifice all the old guilt and shame as part of the Gnostic Divine Surplus of Riches Ritual.

THE GNOSTIC DIVINE SURPLUS OF RICHES RITUAL

As your Gnostic Money Manifesting Ritual starts to pay off, it becomes ever more important that you use this variation to insure that you keep more of your good than would otherwise be the case. If it is a health problem for you or a loved one that is draining your resources, the upcoming work of our health chapter is very much in point, too, but you will find *this* work important to your financial well-being at every stage of your life.

Prepare for this ritual just as you did for the Gnostic Money Manifesting Ritual, but this time write out the chant: 'I lovingly and willingly sacrifice all my guilts and shame about my past money management to Bast, my envy and jealousy of others' riches to Isis, my own lack of riches to Osiris, my ineffectiveness to Ishtar and my disorganization to Abraxas. I gladly accept your gifts of peace, enlightenment, prosperity, effectiveness and organization and pledge their efficient use to vastly improve my financial condition. I invite your guidance in all money management matters and ask your help in producing an ever-increasing divine surplus of riches in my life from this moment on. My loving thanks to all." (And again sign your name exactly as you do on your checks.)

Of course read it with feeling eight times, using the release by fire technique on the eighth reading. And you will do well to slip this into the blank periods of eight days between your money manifesting rituals. Thus each ritual is done for 64 days in alternating eight-day cycles, and we could well describe the combined technique as "128 days to financial security."

Feedback letters from the divine surplus ritual generally read like this: "There always used to be too much month left at the end of the money, but now things are wonderful—I have a comfortable balance in my checking account and a nicely growing savings account, too." But let's share a few with interesting variations. This report from F.Y. shows a potential side effect that is always good for a nice warm glow as well as a financial boost: "I'm retired and didn't see much potential for me in the money manifesting ritual, so I decided to focus all my effort on the money management—divine surplus idea. I got a good feeling on the work during the first eight-day sessions, but it was when I started the second round after the eight-day lay-off period that I got a really wonderful surprise. It was a letter from a friend I had emotionally demoted to acquaintance and had not seen for over five years. I had loaned him money in dribs and drabs for several years before that and finally got tired of it and cut him off at my pockets. Enclosed with the letter was a one-thousand dollar check and a strange sort of thank-you. He said, 'Thanks for cutting me off so I had to stand on my own feet. I'm doing well now and hope this money will repay you for what I cost you before you wised up and cut me off.' My savings account can certainly stand the addition, and it's hard to say which is nicer, the money or the nice feeling about the gesture from my old friend."

J.E. had this perhaps more typical report: " I have grossed well over $50,000 a year in salary and commissions for more years than I care to admit, but I was still one of those people who felt that there was more month than money. I'm getting older now and I was certainly ripe for your Gnostic Divine Surplus Ritual. There's not a simple way to explain the difference, but I was way in debt when I started the ritual work. Now, only about a year later, I have all my bills paid, a nicely growing savings account and 100 shares of a real blue chip stock. And I know that this is only the beginning of the growth of my personal fortune."

DARING TO MAKE IT BIG, QUICKLY

Although I consider myself emotionally, religiously and sexually liberal, I am so conservative financially and politically that when my very southern family migrated to California, I was the first of us to register Republican. That was just about 30 years ago, and my liberal areas have since grown more liberal while my conservative side has grown even more conservative. I offer this background for this section because we will consider those times when a person should momentarily set aside his conservatism and take the plunge. Let me continue with the personal example for a moment. In late 1974 when the gloom and doomers were still in vogue, I got a strong urge to take a position in the stock market. My friends were all sure I was crazy, but it felt right so I invested about 20% of my then net worth in carefully selected common stocks. 1975 turned out to be a good year and I derived about a 65% annual return—a lot better than a savings account. And since then through good years and bad, with a bit of magic and lots of spirit guidance (which we will talk more about later), I have averaged better than a 40% annual return, mostly taxed at the more favorable capital gains rates.

It would have been easy to talk myself out of the market and stay with the "safer" investments with less than 10% returns, but it would have been an insult to my good spirit guidance and the principles of Gnostic Magic. To those who like the wild gamble, this may still sound very conservative, but it was a big and happy step for me, and I hope it will illustrate the principle we're trying to get across. If hard work were really the secret of success, the ditch diggers would own the world—but obviously they don't. There is for each of us a "financial muse," quite in tune with your personal financial philosophy, there to lead and guide you to windfalls and opportunities for relatively big gains. To ignore these promptings would be as defeating to your magic as to refuse to sacrifice your guilts about past mistakes. We will have much more to say about guidance from beings in the unseen realms in our later work, but let's take a moment here to consider "courting your personal financial muse."

By using the classic Greek idea of "muse," we can get right at our work and neatly postpone a discussion of the deeper realities of the thing to a more appropriate time. Right now we are concerned only with hooking you up with a reliable source of solid guidance, both to keep you from big financial mistakes and to lead you to your windfalls and major gains. You won't have to take my word for it—time will certainly prove that YOUR muse is real, by the positive results if nothing else. But you will have to settle for getting your inputs on the "hunch" level in the beginning. The power comes on a growth basis, so the sooner you start to use it, the sooner you will have really magnificent financial help and guidance closer than your fingertips.

THE GNOSTIC QUICKIE FINANCIAL MUSE CONTACT RITE

This one is so quick and easy that we had to call it a rite rather than a ritual. You can use it anywhere on a completely mental level, or prepare with candles and incense at your normal Gnostic workplace. The essence is what counts here: Mentally, but with feeling, sacrifice your confusion to Thoth, ineffectiveness to Ishtar and disorganization to Abraxas, and accept the return gifts of clear communications, effectiveness and organization. Then aloud or mentally ask: "I invite contact with the guidance from my financial muse. Please touch me with a feeling of guidance that we may learn to work effectively together, now." Then sit quietly, but make a careful mental note of the next thing (or few things) you think about.

At first you may not feel that you're picking up the guidance, but just a little practice will give you the feel of it and make it a magnificent tool to enhance all the rest of your financial life. In one or more of the tiny trains of thought after the request for guidance, there will be an urge to buy something, sell something, or a feeling of stand pat for now. For at least the first week it is well to keep these as "practice runs" with no intention of acting on the guidance, but simply proving up the working relationship. If your interest is in stocks, commodities or the like, it is relatively easy to follow the results of your fictitious dry run actions to see if they would have been positive or negative—and sometimes you may get the name of a horse (or a set of numbers), which is also very easy to check out.

If you keep simple notes almost as if it were a scorepad, you will quickly realize that when you got the positive or "winning" inputs, there was a very definite *feeling* that came with them—a sort of calm inner knowing and peace. Similarly, when you picked up an erroneous or incorrect input, there came with it a slightly uneasy feeling almost as if you were being mocked. When you clearly recognize the feeling with each input, you have "automatic throwing out of the bad data" and clear sailing to much fresh success. Your muse may quite often give you the simple stand-pat input during the practice periods, so that in your frustration you will reach out and bring through bad data. This is the only way to get the feeling of the difference between frustration and wishful thinking and a solid input from your muse. Play the game to develop your skills; you can become a very big winner in a very short time!

P.G. sent us this report on his first two weeks of practice: "I started courting my financial muse (or M.M. as I call him, for Money Muse), and played the dry run bit for about a week. Then on Monday morning I saw a three digit number and it felt good so I played it and won a fast $500. And on Wednesday, I felt that I heard the name of a horse. Again it felt good so

I invested a good part of Monday's winnings on it and brought home over $3,000 for my trouble. Not bad for the first few days after only a week's dry run! You're right, Gnostic Magic can clearly be a happy path to riches and joy."

O.T. found his guidance in the stock market, which is perhaps more in point to our work, but no better or worse than any other positive manifestation. Here's what he had to say: "I had bought this one big board stock at 14 and watched it sink slowly to just about 7, and there it seemed to stay. I more or less forgot about it for a while, but asked about it in one of my early practice runs with my financial muse. The stand-pat feeling was very clear on it, and I took the advice, though I had been toying with the idea of dumping the dog and looking for a better investment. Almost at once that stock started to shoot up. When it got back to 14 I was sure it was time to sell, but my muse kept giving me the stand-pat feeling. Believe it or not, I sold at 25¾, which was the stock's absolute peak. Within three days after I sold it, it was back down under 20 and never got over 17 again for the several months I followed it out of curiosity afterwards. There has been lots of other good guidance, but I knew of your interest in the stock market and that hitting the absolute peak on a sale would be meaningful to your feedback program."

GNOSTIC MAGIC MIND JOGGERS

1. To prepare for a big boost in income, spend some time getting better acquainted with money and your ideas about it. Be ready to sacrifice your negative ideas to get ahead.
2. Next spend some time wallowing in the positive feelings and ideas about money; get the feel of being rich—it will help you manifest real riches.
3. Enjoy performing the Gnostic Money Manifesting Ritual, and watch as it helps you to bring wonderful new streams of money and riches into your life.
4. Examine the Gnostic Money Management Principles and start to apply them, then enhance your work with the Gnostic Divine Surplus of Riches Ritual.

5. We could quite properly call the combination of the money manifesting and divine surplus rituals your 128-day path to riches and financial security. Tread it.

6. There are also times to plunge in and make it big. Develop the channels of guidance from your financial muse with the Gnostic Quickie Financial Muse Contact Rite.

7. You're on your way to riches—I'll be watching for a magnificent feedback letter from YOU.

5

The Gnostic Magic Way to Lasting Love and Loyal Friendships

Homo Sapiens (the scientific term for the human species) is a gregarious animal. We human beings are not loners; we need and enjoy the company and cooperation of others of our species, not just for survival, but to give enough meaning to life that we feel it might be worth the struggle to survive. If your every relationship with another human is and has been completely pleasant and rewarding, feel free to bypass this chapter; the rest of us will catch up with you later. Meanwhile, let's get into the meat of ever-improving and more rewarding human relations.

GETTING BETTER ACQUAINTED WITH LOVE AND FRIENDSHIP

Whether you are looking for romance and marriage, or for good personal friendships, there is a powerful Gnostic definition of the right terms for any genuine relationship. Think of it as *two complete beings coming together not out of need but for the sheer joy of sharing experiences together*. We may well make good friends out of our business acquaintances, or even marry one of them (or at least one at a time), but the relationship will be mutually rewarding on the human relations level ONLY as genuine sharing replaces the business aspects in emphasis and importance. So the keynote of the size and scope of friendship is the idea of SHARING. And we should be able to agree that in the same sense love is GIVING—but again if the giving is not mutual, the relationship will quickly deteriorate.

The taste and feel of love and friendship should be delicious. If you have to plan or scheme to get your share of good out of the contacts, you will know that the relationship is neither love nor friendship. Indeed the opposite is true—each person should be comfortable about forgetting his (or her) own interests and looking out for the interests of the partner. When this type of relationship is mutual (but of course not overdone), you find the essence of true friendship, and it should survive "forever."

The color and texture of love/friendship is as varied as are the shadings of the relationships themselves. The base color is the same green that we found in strength and prosperity, but in the love/friendship application it is nicely spiced with Nergal's red and Marduk's blue. Think how a lack of the energy from either of these three chakras would detract from a friendship or love affair. Without Osiris' green energy you lack the power, prosperity and confidence you need to hold up your end; without Nergal's red you lack the energy and animal magnetism to keep it alive; and without Marduk's blue, you lack the creativity and ability to sweep away the negative. But with happy amounts of all three, you are well on your way to creating totally beautiful relationships.

The special spiritual quality of the love/friendship side of our lives is shown in its number, the spiritual seven. This gives us a nice rhythm for planning our magical work. Think of it as one week on and one week off, of course using the ritual chant itself seven times a sitting. We might suggest an added refinement here: for purely platonic relationships, Friday would be the best day to start your week of ritual work, but if you are seeking sexually oriented relationships, Tuesday might be a better starting day. Then for the added power of the repeated rhythm, you might plan seven sets of one week on and one week off.

Let's pause here to answer the obvious question: can I work on more than one set of rituals at a time? For instance, would it be OK to work on both riches and love/friendship? My answer is it all depends on your amount of free time and your motivation. There is nothing at all wrong with running more than one set of rituals as long as you keep a schedule, stick to it, and make all the ritual work fun. If it starts to drag, you know you're doing too much.

HOW TO USE THE GNOSTIC LOVE/FRIENDSHIP RITUAL

As preparation for using this very powerful device to produce much fresh love and friendship, it is well to pause to compare your current actions and attitudes with the discussion of the Gnostic ideals we just finished. Be ready to give up your limiting thought and action patterns as you enter fully into the spirit of the ritual and launch a fresh new life of love and popularity.

Complete your preparation by writing the sacrifice chant in your own hand: "I lovingly and willingly sacrifice my lack of personal magnetism to Nergal, my possessiveness to Bast, my selfishness to Osiris, my ineffectiveness to Ishtar and my disorganization to Abraxas. I gladly accept your gifts of attractiveness, comfort, fulfillment, effectiveness and organization and pledge their efficient application to uplift all areas of my life. And I ask your help in focusing the energies to bring extra love, friendship and companionship to me now. My heartfelt thanks." (Sign it with your normal signature.) Take the paper to your altar or work place, set the mood with candles, incense and your favorite perfume, cologne or love oil, and follow our by now familiar procedure. Hold the paper between your palms while you picture yourself bathed in loving white Light. Then read the sacrifice chant with feeling six times as you strive to honestly give up the negative qualities. Then touch the upper left-hand corner of the paper

to the candle flame and read the chant again just ahead of the flame, and at the end drop the burning paper into the receptacle you have prepared for this part of the work. Sit quietly and soak up the good vibes along with any immediate guidance that may come to you. When you feel finished, thank your energy transformer friends once more, snuff your candles and go back to your normal routine.

Some degree of personal growth is a necessary part of the repeated ritual work, as this report from Lily S. well illustrates: "Jim and I had broken up about six weeks before I started to use the Gnostic Love/Friendship Ritual, and part of my reason for the ritual work was that I had given up hope of ever hearing from him again. I entered into the spirit of the work, and on my second night in quiet meditation after the ritual, I began to fully realize how my selfishness and fierce possessiveness had been the cause of the break in the old relationship. So I promised myself to work especially hard at honestly sacrificing these negative qualities, and I kept at it with vigor and enthusiasm. By the time I started the second week of rituals, I felt I was making really good progress. I even figured out that it was plain old insecurity that had made me so obnoxiously possessive. Then my phone rang. It was Jim. He said he had been thinking about me and would like to start dating again if I would promise not to sharpen my claws. I told him I thought I'd grown up a bit these last couple of months and agreed to a date. I won't make this too long with more details; just let me say that this time it has been a really mutually rewarding relationship—and without any pushing, Jim asked me to marry him. We're wonderfully happy and I feel we know how to KEEP it that way. Thanks."

John N. reported: "When my company transferred me to this new town I realized I didn't know ANYBODY. And since I am quite shy by nature it stayed that way, and I was virtually a complete loner for just about a year. You can imagine my delight at finding the Gnostic Love/Friendship Ritual. I began to use it with enthusiasm and feeling. By the end of the third night's session, there were noticeable results. People who had ignored me for a year began to smile at me and greet me with a 'hello' or something. That week I got three dinner invitations from three different families, each of whom wanted me to meet a relative or close friend who was also lonely. Let's just say that my social life went from zilch to wildly active almost overnight. I've been dating quite a few girls now and am in the process of narrowing down the field with the thought of marriage in a few more months. I never thought I'd have a wide choice of girls like this, either. It's wonderful!"

HOW TO HANDLE THE LOVE AND ADMIRATION THAT WILL INEVITABLY BE HEAPED UPON YOU

As John N's report clearly indicates, proper use of the Gnostic Love/Friendship Ritual will bring some pretty major changes into your life. There are also unsettling aspects to this, in particular a tendency toward a big ego trip. When people are making a big happy fuss over you, it is important to realize at once that they are responding to the new power in your aura that was put there by a JOINT effort of you AND your friendly energy transformer personalities. All too often the occult student will begin to get "fantastic" results, then get so wrapped up in the fun of the manifestations that he (or she) forgets what was causing it. So he slowly slips back into his old set of bad habits and adds a couple of new ones to boot. Then, to borrow my pet phrase in our classes, "When you're picking yourself up off the floor, don't bemoan the fickleness of fate. Instead get down on your knees and say, 'Gee, thanks guys, I needed that put-down to get back on the right track!'"

Then go right back to your fundamentals and promise yourself that this time you won't forget what is causing your success. Obviously this discussion belongs in every chapter of this book because success in any area of your life does tend to distract you from the work that brings it about. The major reason that we seem to get our progress in spurts followed by flat periods or really down ones is the subtle changes in US. The only way to insure regular progress is to be nimble enough to keep your balance even in the face of exaggerated admiration or virtually unlimited new wealth. And the essence of the balance is your continued special relations with the energy transformer personalities coupled with the humility that KNOWS you didn't really get there by yourself. I could give you lots of examples of the roller coaster type of life, but there is no reason to waste your time on them. Just try to be aware of your changing attitudes, and if you should slip, know at once what to do to get back into the mainstream of your growth.

BALANCING THE RESPONSIBILITIES OF LOVE AND FRIENDSHIP WITH THE RESPONSIBILITY TO YOURSELF

There are many traps in the deeper interpersonal relationships, particularly where there is a bit too much immaturity in your friend or loved one. The classic examples that come to mind here are the badly hung-over daughter staggering into the family room in the early afternoon of a Sunday and opening with, "Mother, if you love me, you'll fix my breakfast," or the equally exasperating situation when mother has just received an unexpected gift and daughter says, "Oh! That's lovely. Can I have it?" But the mother/daughter relationship is no more fraught with such pitfalls than any other—there is always the friend whose need is the lever used to impose on you or sap your sustenance in one way or another. It is important to recognize these assults as direct breaches of the love/friendship relationship and have the confidence to politely refuse.

Remember that the ONLY reason to help another person is that YOU WANT to, never because of pressure or the other person's "need." Your first responsibility must always be to yourself, otherwise you will soon have no means to care for anyone. Take care to understand this and not let it in any way detract from your sense of personal worthiness. To appear before your energy transformer friends to ask for help because you are in trouble after squandering your resources in weakness or a vain attempt to buy admiration or friendship makes

you look exceedingly foolish. We earn the respect and enthusiasm of the higher beings who can really help us by demon-
strating STRENGTH, not weakness.

And there is the added responsibility of true love or
friendship not to act to weaken the other being. To give in to
pressure is to encourage the weakness and habits of manip-
ulating people in your "friend." This would be as bad a breach
of the relationship as to be the one applying the pressure. Let's
promise ourselves to recognize the pressures and accept them
as challenges to us to have the courage to stand fast and say
"NO." Every time you do, you are participating actively in
your own process of growth.

THE JOY OF FRIENDSHIP WITH NON-HUMAN CREATURES

As you regularly use the Gnostic Love/Friendship Ritual,
it is natural that you will also excite the interest of fascinating
creatures not belonging to the human species. Even in our big
cities we humans are in a tiny minority compared to the birds,
insects and other creatures who have adapted to our surroundings with obvious ease. There are several excellent reasons to
allow yourself to develop a working rapport with at least a few
of your nearby "little friends." First should be the sheer
enjoyment of this new form of truly shared experience;
second you will find that it does wonderful things for your
insights into yourself and the workings of the "real world"
around you; but of tremendous importance to a budding
magician is the fact that the little furry and crawly friends are
a direct link to the power and friendship of the nature spirits
and elementals. And no matter how sloppy your ritual work,
with the loving help of nature spirits and elementals, I can
guarantee that your magic will bring you wonderfully good
results!

Many people talk to their pet dogs and cats and feel that
they are well understood, but have you considered that a fly,
an ant, or even a cockroach can understand you with equal
ease? In all these cases your thoughts and feelings reach the

"lower" being readily, so it is really a problem of YOU learning to receive from them. We will spend some effort on this because the principles will be of inestimable value to all the rest of your magical work.

How will you receive clear and direct communication from a small being who has no voice or ability to write? Clearly the way is a communion of feeling reasonably well described by the ideas of empathy and rapport. And such a state can only be established by loving interest and consideration. Let's pause here to consider a real life example from a young salesman who had been working to build a rapport with the nature spirits through all "lower" forms of life. Here is what he said: "We have two bathrooms which we call hers and his. Mine is at the far end of the house and I use it to shower in the morning. While I'm showering, shaving, etc., my wife gets up and starts breakfast. This particular morning I went into my wife's bathroom to pick up a cake of soap. As I was opening the cabinet I noticed that the wash basin was literally covered with ants. I thought of this as a potential tragedy, so I spoke aloud to them, saying: 'Look fellas, I know it's really none of my business, but if you guys are here like this when my wife comes in, she'll kill all of you. If I were you, I'd get out of here right away.' I said it with real loving concern, then went on to my bathroom to start my morning routine. When I got to the kitchen later I was curious, so I asked my wife, 'How did you make out with the ants?' She replied, 'What ants?' When she had arrived in the bathroom just about ten minutes after I left it, there was not one ant to be seen! I left the house with a nice warm glow, and some may say coincidence, but I know better. I made more money that one day in sales than I had made for the whole two weeks before! You're right! It really pays to work for a loving rapport with nature's creatures."

But that shows only the attitude necessary in *you* to be able to get real two-way communication going with your creature friends. We also need to work on your receiving apparatus. The biggest single hurdle is to decide that you're "crazy" enough to talk to an insect or small animal and

honestly *expect* to get an intelligent answer. Yet this is not
nearly such a stretch of one's three-dimensionally oriented
mind as talking to a watch or comb and having it tell you
many things about its owner, as we can all do in the practice
known as *psychometry*. In either case the biggest step is your
DECISION to really try it. Once that decision is made, simply
focus your attention and love on the creature in question, give
it a friendly "Hi!" and perhaps ask it a question or comment
on something you feel may be of mutual interest. Then
quietly "listen," NOT for a voice, but simply for an answering
thought inside your head.

Here the beginner's instant reaction is, "How can I tell if
it's the bug talking or just my imagination?" Let's answer
with the frankness that admits that at first there is no way to
be *sure*. But with practice, an occasional tidbit of information
you get that way can be really checked out and you will get
the "feel" of it. This is on the same level as learning to bake
biscuits or a cake from scratch—at first you're not at all sure
how it's going to turn out, but with some experience behind
you your batting average improves to near perfection. Let's
expand our field of communication to include your house
plants as well as the more mobile small creatures around you
and look at some reports of the benefits of working to build
the two-way rapport.

LET'S LEARN BY EXAMPLE

Dorothy S. is a widow who was finding it very hard to run
her little house on her $240-a-month social security check
and her tiny remaining savings. She loved the house and the
little creatures around it, and always kept her bird feeder
stocked with seeds, considering them just as important as her
own food supplies. Dorothy was at the point of listing her
loved home for sale to make ends meet when she got some
quite unexpected help. We will let her continue: "Thank you
for the wonderful suggestion of a two-way rapport with the
creatures around me. The wild birds who enjoy my bird feeder
have long ago accepted me and will go about their business of

eating and playing while I sit in the yard very close to them. The day after I got the two-way idea, I sat in my chair and began to project love to the birds. One saucy blue one very quickly flew over and landed on the ground about two feet in front of me. I said, 'Hi, pretty friend, I sure enjoy your company.'

"Then something inside me sort of popped and I poured out my heart to the pretty bird, saying how much I would miss all my feathered friends when I had to give up my house. As I talked, he seemed to nod in understanding quite often. Then I felt I owed him an apology for burdening him with my troubles, but when I started to say 'I'm sorry' to him, I'll swear he gave me a great big wink and flew away. Within an hour my phone rang, and as a friend was inviting me to be her guest at the local horse race track next afternoon, there was my same bluebird pecking at the window sill and nodding his head up and down. I had thought not to accept since I know nothing about racehorses, but I let the bluebird talk me into it. And I had a feeling that he would help. Next morning I took my paper out into the garden to browse and watch my bird friends. And here came that bluebird. Somehow I knew that he intended to help me pick the horses, so I turned to that section in the paper and began to read aloud the horses' names. Occasionally the bird would chirp loudly or sort of hop up and down. Each time, I marked the name of the horse I had just read. When my friend came to pick me up, she saw I had marked the program in my paper and asked if I had a system. I couldn't resist the reply, 'No, a little bird told me,' of course with a smile on my face so she wouldn't think I'm completely crazy.

"And what a magnificent day it was. I won the first race, the daily double and second race, and had five out of six winners in the first six races. I came home with a little over $1,200 and some special treat food for the birds. Now my friend wants to take me every day, but we decided that any time I want to go, I'll just call her and she'll drop everything to take me. I don't want to overtax my bluebird friend, and I'm not greedy but we go often enough to keep comfortably ahead of the financial squeeze. Al, my bird friends saved my home for me! But even more wonderful is the new truly magical relationship we have. It's the nicest thing an old lady could ever dream of!"

Of course you don't have to be "needy" to have the magic of friendship with the "little creatures" give you a big lift. John E. was already quite a successful business man when he bought a nice house in a rustic area of a big city. One of the big features of the property for John and his family had been the lovely half-acre orchard just full of beautiful fruit trees. Here is his report: "What a disappointment it was! I spent the whole time battling the birds and squirrels for the fruit from these wonderful trees—but I was clearly losing. I was thinking of buying all kinds of electronic and mechanical gadgets to drive away the squirrels and birds, but never quite got around to it. Then I was doing the Gnostic Love/Friendship ritual one Sunday morning and the idea hit me to go out and sit in the orchard to see if I could make some sort of a deal for at least part of my fruit. I took a chair, set myself up comfortably right in the middle of things and began projecting love to the creatures.

"In about a half-hour I watched as a whole family of squirrels came under my chain link fence and started raiding a fruit-laden tree (it always griped me that they would unvaryingly get the fruit about three days before I figured it would be ripe enough to pick!). I was sitting very still and what looked like the father squirrel stopped to look at me. I softly said, 'Hey, fellow, how come you guys think you can take all my fruit like that? I don't think it's fair.' As the little squirrel blinked at me I was struck with a new bit of insight. It was as if he had spoken inside my head, 'You have plenty of money to afford to buy your own fruit, but this is our only source of livelihood.' Then I had a strong impulse to battle no more. It was as if the squirrel had said: 'You take good care of our trees and leave us the fruit—we'll see that you prosper in other ways.' So I went back to the house and told my family just that. 'We'll let our little friends have that fruit and I'll stick to business to be sure we are well provided for in the ways I do best.' Al, almost overnight my business literally doubled with a corresponding five-fold increase in net profits! Lucky breaks and windfall profits seem almost to rain down on me. We are at peace with the creatures of the orchard and put out food for them during the times the vines and trees are not bearing. It's a much happier life, too, living in peace with our tiny neighbors—it makes the inside of the house much more loving also. There has never been a time when we have been so happy as a family."

Love, friendship, fullfillment and all manner of tangible help from the realm of the nature spirits are right there waiting for YOU. Even if you feel "silly" about it at first, go ahead and make the first move—your non-human friends will prove helpful beyond the limits of your imagination.

GNOSTIC MAGIC MIND JOGGERS

1. Study the Gnostic principles of love and friendship to prepare yourself to effectively sacrifice your negative habits and feelings to improve all of your human relations.
2. Then use the Gnostic Love/Friendship Ritual and launch a fresh new life of love and popularity.
3. You will find a natural emotional and spiritual growth from regular use of the ritual; it will bring you many happy side benefits as it uplifts your every relationship.
4. Take care to avoid the tendency toward an ego trip as your ritual work brings you the many benefits. Always remember what caused your new and happy situation and keep up the good work with your energy transformer friends.
5. Learn to accept the responsibility to yourself and others and have the confidence to say NO where it is proper.
6. There is much growth and tangible help that results from extending your love/friendship to include the tiny creatures within your environment. Befriending and building a working rapport with your plants or small animals will open the door for help from the elementals and nature spirits, with wonderfully happy results. Try it and be a big winner.

6

Secret Gnostic Rituals for Perfect Health

In our last chapter we spoke of success and its strong tendency to distract you from the practices that produced it. This is certainly true of health; when we have it, the natural thing to do is ignore it and thus sow the seeds for future physical discomfort. Let's have a good look at the Gnostic approach to attaining and maintaining perfect health, then apply it to stay radiantly healthy and full of zest and the enjoyment of life.

GETTING ACQUAINTED WITH VIBRANT HEALTH

At this point in our research class work at E.S.P. Lab I made a tongue-in-cheek suggestion to the group: to get a really good perspective on your life, go out and get falling down drunk; then next morning while you're lying there suffering, you'll realize that the health and vitality of your body comes first—without that, all the magnificent things you're striving for in the material world become completely empty and meaningless. Hopefully your memory will suffice so you can avoid the actual physical discomfort, but a bit of reflection on your last period of any kind of physical indisposition will remind you of the size and scope of our practice of perfect health—it is the first principle of *any* lasting success.

But what are the causes of good health? Long before modern scientific aura research showed that disease appears in the auric or energy bodies many hours, days or even weeks before the first physical symptoms, the Gnostic Magicians knew and taught the same truths. To the Gnostic, the physical body is a focal point for the dynamic flow of the universal psychic and emotional energies, and when these are in proper balance, vibrant health is the natural result. Let's state a simple Gnostic law: THE NATURAL STATE OR CONDITION OF YOUR PHYSICAL BODY IS VIBRANT HEALTH. In the event of discomfort or disease, it is necessary to find the energy blocks and restore their natural flow, then the body will automatically return to its natural state—HEALTH.

So we need to look at the causes of the energy blocks that always precede a physical difficulty. Our clue can be found in an ancient saying, "Whom the Gods would destroy they first make mad." The word *mad* can mean either angry or crazy, but in the higher sense there is little difference. The meaning comes through that it is our negative emotions and reactions that cause blocks and distortions of the normal health energy flow patterns. The "modern" ideas of psychosomatic medicine follow a weaker version of the same ideas—that ulcers, hives, and even the common cold are quite generally recognized today as being emotionally caused—but this literally only scratches the surface.

Now I'm not going to tell you that the secret of perfect health is never to get angry or resentful again! If I did I would be giving you an impossible solution. We're all human and regularly run into situations that lead us to generate negative emotional reactions. True, EVERY negative reaction releases some degree of poison into your physical system, but your body is set up to eliminate reasonable amounts of these with essentially no deterioration or debilitation of the organism. It is HOW YOU HANDLE your negative reactions that maintains your health or makes you sick!

Rheumatism and consumption were big bugaboos in olden times, to which we should add cancer and arthritis today as ailments brought on by suppressed rage and resentment. Note the word *suppressed* (or should we borrow the psychological term, repressed?) as the key here. A popular TV program made the word "stifle" a household term for the same thing, and helps to stress the danger of the action. A strong emotion is (or produces) a tremendous amount of energy that MUST be worked off in a constructive way if it is not to injure the body. To stifle or block it will totally disrupt all of your healthy energy flow patterns. Here we are reminded of the Bible verse: "If thy brother trespass against thee, rebuke him. And if he repent, forgive him." That sounds easy, but what if he's "bigger" than you (physically or within the power structure) and tells you to go straight to hell? Then you have a challenge to be truly creative in working off the energy of resentment. If you haven't found a constructive outlet, go to your altar and ask Marduk to help you burn up your present resentment and guide you to a viable long-run solution.

Similarly, anxiety-produced tensions, unrelieved, are the cause of strokes, heart attacks, or the premature aging (wearing out) of the body. These and related diseases are often the plague of the big achiever, but tension is not limited to highly successful people. Here believers in reincarnation have a strong advantage; when any problem is viewed from the perspective of many lifetimes, it is easier to reduce its tension/emotional content. But with or without thinking of past and future lives, you must learn enough about yourself to turn off the tension switch and work off the excess bottled-up energy.

We could spend a whole book on the details of emotional energy flow and health, but our purpose here is just to get you thinking this way, so you can clearly recognize the negative thought/emotion/reaction patterns you will have to sacrifice to receive the gift of perfect health in return.

UPDATING THE GNOSTIC CONTEXT OF
PERFECT HEALTH

We are dealing with a system that worked magnificently at the time of the Gnostics, and which will work equally well for you now. But a bit of updating of the context to take into account changes in the patterns of civilization is in order. In the preceding section, there was no mention of diet, for instance. But look at the Gnostic setting—from Pythagoras to the second century A.D., there was nothing to resemble our processed and highly refined foods. Rough foods, just as nature made them, were the only available items to eat. Thus a well-adjusted Gnostic Magician could rely on his appetites to provide his body with its necessary nutrients. If there was a missing element, he could depend on his body to develop a "craving" for these foods that would supply its needs. And within limits that is true today. The major exception, of course, is a craving for sweets.

In our modern society, the most popular reward foods are candy, cookies, cake and the like. Thus when morale is low, there could be a strong craving for the sweets because they are associated on the subliminal or preconscious level with approval and acceptance; to satisfy this kind of craving is to add unneeded weight to the physical body while adding to the cause of the lowered morale. It is essential that you understand the principles of good nutrition and be prepared to sacrifice your unhealthy eating patterns along with your negative emotions as you prepare to accept the gift of perfect health.

Another updating of context should consider the pace of life itself. The great technological advances of the modern age have brought us much in the way of creature comforts and efficiency of labor, but with these have come a more and more frantic pace in our lives. In the Gnostic times, news traveled very slowly, and indeed nothing happened very fast. Thus there was a greater natural peace and serenity within which to perform one's ritual work, and there was time to enjoy the loveliness of the spirit and nature spirit responses. So if we are to get the maximum value from our ritual work, we must also think in terms of sacrificing the fast pace of our daily life, at least for the period of time set aside for our magical work.

TIMING AND SETTING THE MOOD FOR YOUR GNOSTIC PERFECT HEALTH RITUAL

Traditionally, Magicians use moon phases and signs and the planetary hours system for timing their ritual work. (If you would like more detail in this area, see the trouble-shooting chapter of my book, *Helping Yourself with White Witchcraft*.) But the most important and indeed the overriding consideration in timing a health ritual is how *you* feel. I have teased about negative timing for years, saying with far too much accuracy that the beginner feels pressed for money, so he does a prosperity ritual and multiplies his bills; he feels lonely so he does a love/friendship ritual and multiplies his loneliness; or he feels sick so he does a health ritual and makes himself sicker! We must always keep in mind the fact that your dominant mood is what actually powers your ritual work, and the manifestation will invariably be the natural result of multiplying that mood and bringing the product into material manifestation.

Thus the key to timing a health ritual is to feel better than you have in a while. Even if you are suffering from a chronic illness, there are days when you feel better than usual, or times in a day when there is a feeling of improvement. If you don't have a feeling of vibrant health to take to your altar, take the next best thing—a feeling that you are better than you have been, or in other words a feeling of POSITIVE PROGRESS. The best idea is to get things ready for your health ritual, wait until the mood is right, then take it to your altar and KNOW that you're going to win.

Preparation for the Gnostic Perfect Health Ritual should begin as if you were preparing for the ritual of joy as we used it in our second chapter. Indeed, so important is the mood and the fun that the perfect health ritual begins with that ritual of joy. The next part of your preparation should be contemplation of your attitudes and emotion/reaction patterns so that you will be ready to willingly sacrifice the negative ones in exchange for better health. The opening section of this chapter was designed just to get you thinking about emotions and health, with the idea that you will realize the specifics as you digest these ideas over a period of several days. If you're not sure you're ready on this point, question your last several stray pains or times of feeling way below par; ask them what caused them, and be alert to notice the defensive feeling that follows—a feeling of needing to defend some emotion or action—then you will be sure that it is the culprit.

The last bit of preparation is to handwrite the health sacrifice affirmation just as we have done with the sacrifice work in previous chapters. The perfect health sacrifice affirmation should read like this: "I lovingly and willingly sacrifice my negative thought/emotion patterns to Marduk, my psychosomatic symptoms to Negral, my resentments to Ra, my ineffectiveness to Ishtar and my disorganization to Abraxas. I gladly accept your gifts of creative peace, physical vitality, happiness, strength, effectiveness and organization and pledge their efficient use in uplifting all areas of my life. And I ask your help to focus these wonderful gifts to create and maintain my perfect health. My heartfelt thanks." (Then sign it with your normal signature.)

Then when the mood is just right, head for your altar and have a happy go at it.

HOW TO USE THE GNOSTIC PERFECT HEALTH RITUAL

The emphasis is on good fellowship and enjoyment as you begin this work with the basic ritual of joy. But instead of meditating just on the qualities and attributes of each individual energy transformer personality, after you finish the salutation and sharing of food and drink, ask aloud, "What special sacrifice may I make to you in conjunction with my health ritual?" Then be silent for at least 30 seconds to feel the answer deep within your being.

When you have completed the joy ritual part, pick up your prepared sacrifice affirmation, hold it between your hands and picture yourself bathed in loving white Light. The proper number for health is ten, so the standard procedure would be to read the affirmation aloud nine times, then touch the upper left-hand corner to your candle flame, and read it the tenth time just ahead of the flame. But if you feel it is finished before that, go ahead and cut the reading short—or lengthen the number of times if the spirt moves you in that direction. As always, make a sincere effort in your heart to honestly give up the negatives the words say you are sacrificing. To the extent that you really turn loose of the negative patterns, the ritual will bring you ever more outstanding success.

Jerimiah I. suffered from chronic back pains in spite of all the medical help, bed boards and chiropractic help he could find. The pain still kept him from sleeping more than two or three hours at a time before having to get up to seek relief from the growing discomfort. Here is his report on using the Gnostic Perfect Health Ritual: "When I was involved with the joy part, talking things over with Ishtar, Nergal and friends, it became apparent that I had to give up my utter disgust with the government and the postal system (which had cost me a lot of money by misdelivering a few key letters), as well as my habit of having an aching back. There were lots of other lesser pet peeves and aggravations to sacrifice also, but I won't give them the dignity of being mentioned here. Suffice it to say that the sacrifice ritual felt almost bloody—I was cutting away so many nasty emotions that had been part of me. That night, I slept all the way through until morning for the first time in 14 years! I knew I wasn't quite finished, so I repeated the whole ritual for nine more nights, bleeding a bit less with each one as I got the mound of negative emotions whittled down to pint size. It has now been three months since I lost any sleep with my back. That's nice enough, but my energy level and zest for life are so much improved that my friends all say I look 25 years younger. When they say that, I agree—I feel 25 years younger, too."

C.C. had this to report: "I really needed the Gnostic Perfect Health Ritual! On the third day of using it, I passed one of my kidney stones, so large the doctors could not believe that I had no trouble passing it. And when I had X-rays taken yesterday (the seventh day of my ritual), they could not find the other one; it had just disappeared. So now I have none left. And as a nice side effect I also got a terrific promotion offer from a company located out of state. It's so good I may take it."

Nothing is impossible, even in the face of serious tissue damage, as this report from N.Y. quite clearly indicates: "In March of last year I encountered your Gnostic Magic work. It appealed to me as a possible way to develop my aura vision. The perfect health ritual seemed to be the proper vehicle, so I tried it. At first I didn't seem to be getting anywhere, so I made a careful point of asking Thoth, Marduk and Nergal for special help in this. I practiced daily for about three months, and slowly I began to see bits and pieces of my aura.

"Then the other day I went to my optometrist for a routine examination. To the surprise and amazement of both of us, my 'normal' vision has improved over 50% and is better than it has ever been. He could not believe this as I injured my eye when I was five years old and the tissues have been damaged ever since. Then later an astigmatism developed. The optometrist could not find it within himself to believe that my vision has improved so much because the tissue of the left eye is still damaged and the astigmatism is still present. He even gave me the test three times, then asked what I had been doing with my eyes. I said I have been sitting for psychic development exercises to see my aura by the instruction of Dr. Al Manning at E.S.P. Laboratory. I even told him how I can now read in the dark. He was astonished and said, 'I'm glad your vision has been improved, but don't touch me under any circumstances.' I found this hilarious. The result of this experience is that my aura vision still needs more work, but my regular vision has increased to such a point that now I only need one pair of glasses and these will be much less magnified. Thanks, Al, and I'll keep at it to get rid of the last pair of glasses and get my good aura vision, too."

HOW TO ADAPT THE GNOSTIC PERFECT HEALTH RITUAL TO HELP A FRIEND OR LOVED ONE

Your own health is of paramount importance, but at times almost insignificant when you are witnessing the suffering of a friend or loved one. It would be mockery indeed if you learned to help yourself but could do nothing to share the health-giving energies with others. Certainly the Gnostic Magicians of old recognized this, thus the adaptations to help others come down to us as well-tested and proved methods.

Naturally the best way to help another is to get him (or her) to join you in the Gnostic Perfect Health Ritual, making it a joint effort with the added power that always comes from group work (even a group of two is much more powerful than the sum of each working individually). But what of those times when the patient is physically unable to participate, or as may be more often the case, what if he is an unbeliever or even fiercely opposed to any form of magical work? All is not lost; you can still help. If at all possible, acquire a picture or handwriting sample of the patient, or any object that belongs to him to use as a sympathetic stand-in for him. If you have nothing tangible, your own clearest mental picture of the person will have to do, but only after you try your best to get an article or picture without attracting undue attention.

Take the picture or article with you to your altar, along with the handwritten sacrifice affirmation, modified to read: "As [*insert the patient's name*] I lovingly and willingly sacrifice my negative . . . " and end it by signing the patient's name and under it, "By [*your name*]." Then during the ritual of joy part ask each energy transformer personality for special extra help for the patient. And when you are ready, read the sacrifice affirmation for your friend or loved one with the same feeling of honest cooperation as you would for yourself. Take care to keep all of the work lighthearted and fun, in spite of your deep attachment to and concern for the patient. Remember that to try hard is self-defeating; it must be a happy experience for the energy transformer personalities and any other visiting spirits if it is to bring the desired results.

SYMPAthetic STAND iN

The ritual will work real "miracles" even under quite adverse conditions, as this report from F.W. demonstrates: "I have been in the hospital with my mother. She had a stroke, then she had another one last week. She was in very critical condition and the doctor told us he couldn't do anything more for her; he obviously expected her to pass over very soon. Even though I didn't have any supplies with me, I knew that I had to do something. So I prepared a sacrificial affirmation for mother, and sat at her bedside going through the complete Gnostic Perfect Health Ritual for her mostly in my imagination, but at least I could read the affirmation aloud. The next morning mother was conscious for the first time in a week. She told me that she had seen a gleaming blue Light that bathed her with its rays and made her feel good. Even before the previous stroke she couldn't talk or eat, but that morning after the ritual she spoke to me and I gave her some coffee and she drank it with enjoyment. The doctor told me it was a miracle—he said he couldn't believe it. Now after 37 days the doctor told me that Dad and I can take her home. She was paralyzed, but now she can move her hands and arms, and she can even stand to get into her wheelchair. As I can now get her to join me in the ritual, I expect to have her quite back to normal in another month."

And this report from the husband of one of our students shows how well the ritual works when you can get your patient's cooperation: "Most of my adult life I have lived with constant pain in my neck and shoulder muscles, due supposedly to nervous tension and stress, the doctors told me, but they never could help me. I was skeptical as all get out but at the same time ready to try anything when my wife suggested that I join her in what I thought was some sort of a ridiculous mystical rite. But she said it would be fun and I could tease her all through the thing if it would make me enjoy it and DO it. I'll admit I was somewhat curious about her carryings-on anyway and I knew that she had somehow produced several strokes of exceptionally good luck, so I reluctantly said OK. I started out making funny faces at my wife when it was time to read the sacrifice affirmation, but her only reaction was to smile and read on. With that kind of good humor as an example I had little choice but to join her. And as I sort of jokingly read it for the third time, my neck started going through what I can only describe as a series of popping and cracking all by itself! I swear to you I did NOT make this happen. I have always twisted my head to pop my neck to relieve tightness, but THIS was *different*. At first I was really worried, I must admit even scared—I thought that someone was taking umbrage about my teasing the ritual and making my condition worse. How can I tell you? Before a week was over I realized that an impossible thing had happened! I was completely free of pain! I used to be afraid the pain would come back, but now I KNOW it won't. Thank you for leading my wife into this work. I have ridiculed it in the past, but now I am encouraging her to study and learn more. In fact, with your good-natured approach, I'll admit that I'm doing a bit of it myself now."

HOW TO ADD EXTRA POWER TO YOUR HEALING WORK FOR OTHERS

Good Gnostic healing work often includes a form of the classic religious technique of the laying on of hands. As a good Gnostic Magician, you know that your hands are transmitters and receivers of the auric energies. Indeed, your two hands held with palms toward each other naturally generate warmth much like the two pads of a diathermy machine. When you have finished the Gnostic Perfect Health Ritual for another person, you will add to the power considerably by applying the energy from your hands directly to the afflicted area. If the patient is present and cooperative, the best approach is to hold one hand on each side of the problem area—almost but not quite touching the skin. Then direct the healing energy to flow, and feel it rinsing and renewing the cells and tissues as it flows. You can also apply the energy in this manner to any sluggish chakra (or all of them) to boost your patient's vitality level. If you are restricted to a photograph or small article, hold it between your hands and image the complete physical practice. In any case, AS SOON AS YOU HAVE FINISHED, GO WASH YOUR HANDS IN COOL WATER to break any possible backwash of energy that would otherwise bring some of the symptoms to you.

There are also times when you can apply the laying on of hands principle to help yourself, as this report from K.J. helps to show: "I am quite an active person with a full schedule, much of which involves using my hands a lot. One day last week I got involved with a faulty furnace in my house and badly burned two fingers of my left hand. As I jerked my hand away from the unexpectedly hot surface, I could see deep blisters, almost four inches long, forming on the index and middle fingers. This was certainly a time for magical action. I put my right hand around the fingers and began willing the flow of healing energy while I asked calmly aloud for special help from Marduk, Nergal, Ishtar and Osiris. For a few moments, I reviewed my last ritual of joy in my mind and carried its feeling into as much as I could remember of the healing sacrifice affirmation ritual. After about five minutes it suddenly dawned on me that there was no more pain—quite a switch because it really hurt like hell at first. So I very slowly opened my right hand to get a look at those burned fingers. AND THEY WERE NOT EVEN RED! The healing was complete and perfect in just about five minutes. I sure said lots of happy thank-you's to the energy transformer personalities for making me so comfortable and helping me not to miss even one day's work."

GNOSTIC MAGIC MIND JOGGERS

1. Your health is your most important single asset. It should be easy to maintain because the natural state or condition of the human body is vibrant health.
2. Diseases and sicknesses are visible in the auric energy field around your body for many hours or even weeks before there are any physical symptoms. Thus disease starts in the psychic part of you and can be healed by good Gnostic Magic.

3. Study the examples of negative thought/reaction and patterns and their suggested physical symptoms; relate this to your own set of emotional patterns and be ready to sacrifice the negative ones before they get a chance to do you any more harm.
4. Remember the historical context that may emphasize the value of rough and non-processed foods in a healthy Magician's diet.
5. Time your health rituals to multiply your feelings of greatest vitality; recognize the Gnostic secret of good timing that works "backward" from the way the average person goes about such things.
6. Use the Gnostic Perfect Health Ritual and enjoy the benefits of healing, renewed vitality and zest for life.
7. You can adapt the perfect health ritual to help others also—either by working together or in their absence, or even without their knowledge.
8. The extra power from applying energy by the direct laying on of hands will add much effectiveness to a Gnostic Magician's healing work.

7

Defeat the Evil Eye or Psychic Attack with Gnostic Power

Please don't let it frighten you, but I'm sure it's accurate to say that YOU are subject to some degree of psychic attack EVERY DAY. Let's take a good look at the degrees of psychic attack and the physical, material and psychological symptoms it produces.

MOST PSYCHIC ATTACK IS UNINTENTIONAL

If someone takes a gun and shoots you deliberately, or if you happen to be a totally innocent bystander and get hit by a stray bullet, the net effect on your body is exactly the same— you've been shot, period. And it is much the same with what we might call the garden variety psychic attack. If you enter a room where two people have just had a violently emotional argument or fight, there will be a lot of negative residue which will attack your aura, lessening its brightness and weakening your psychic and physical organisms. Or if you must remain in the presence of someone who is angry, you are under somewhat more direct attack—and if the person is angry at YOU, the psychic attack becomes quite severe. Beyond the garden variety of attack, we must also consider those situa-

Negative Residue

tions where you are under attack from another "magician" who may be using vicious attack spells deliberately directed to mess up your life expression or even to destroy your physical body. Here, too, there are degrees of attack, depending upon the proficiency and effectiveness of the attacker.

Obviously the greatest percentage of attack to which you may be subjected is the garden variety—that is, it is quite unintentional on the overt level (although your adversary may well enjoy the thought of your potential discomfort). Thus we will focus most of our effort on the gentleness that removes the unintentional attack energy without harming anyone. But we will also give you a good reversing ritual to use to turn the tables on a deliberate attacker in those rare cases where it becomes necessary.

There may also be varying degrees of attempts to control you (or sell you something) that range from the open and honest to flat-out psychic attack. In all of these cases it is important to recognize the attack while it is still on the psychic level and has not yet had a chance to do physical or psychological damage. This is a subtle study that is best begun with a better look at the symptoms or manifestations it causes.

HOW TO RECOGNIZE THE SYMPTOMS OF PSYCHIC ATTACK

Feeling slightly out of sorts? "Mad" for no apparent reason? Are you making more than your normal number of silly mistakes? Have you stumbled or cut yourself for no good reason? Have "little coincidences" managed to keep you from a big sale or from meeting the right person? Have you had more than your share of "bad luck" recently? Does it seem as though the world doesn't like you any more? A *yes* answer to any of these questions is indicative, and two or more *yes* answers is just about a certainty, that you are under a serious degree of psychic attack. There is a very fine line here between practical truth and paranoia; on the other hand, an occasional extra psychic defense ritual doesn't cost much either in time or in supplies, so at least at first it may be better to overdo than not to do enough.

As you progress in the Gnostic magical work, you will build a proficiency that will enable you to recognize a negative thoughtform, tell it it's not for you, and send it on out of your experience—all within the space of five to ten seconds. But even here, good psychic ecology requires that you not let strongly negative thoughtforms go on to cause trouble somewhere else. One's sense of responsibility to the community would require that you break up or destroy them before they breed more of their kind by causing similar troubles for other people.

I used one of my pet terms, "psychic ecology," here because it is in itself a major defense against the random or garden variety of psychic attack. When you keep your aura and the whole psychic atmosphere around you as clean as possible, many of the would-be attacking energy fields will avoid your proximity. It is simply too clean for them to enter comfortably, so they look for the muddier psychic atmosphere that is more to their liking, somewhere else! And in this sense, you will gradually become aware of your aura just as you are of your hands. If your hands get dirty, you feel it and wash them. Similarly, you will be aware of psychic dirt in your aura and clean it, thus protecting your psychic health in much the same way you protect your physical health—with reasonably good habits of cleanliness.

Let's try to understand the mechanism a bit better so we can see how to cope with it. First there are few if any "magicians" who are powerful enough to "do you in" in one quick stroke. Negative magic, like its happily positive counterparts, works mostly on the principle of a small force working virtually unopposed and continuously until it piles up the necessary clout to manifest its victory. It is analogous in operation to the ancient Chinese water torture as opposed to a knife or gun, but left unchecked it can ruin your material life and/or fill your physical body with pain and sickness, causing it finally to waste away to nothing. And again in analogy, it starts rather like a pregnancy; a very small bit of programmed life energy (unfortunately programmed in the wrong way) attaches itself to you and draws upon your own life energy for its sustenance as it grows big enough to enter into physical manifestation. And again as in an unwanted pregnancy, abortion or miscarriage, it is relatively safe and harmless in the very early stages, but grows more difficult and dangerous as the attacking energy field grows. Thus you will see why I recommend a good psychic cleansing about once a week, just in case you've picked up something you are not aware of—and of course always immediately after you know you have been subjected to psychic attack. Perhaps the best way to learn more on this subject is to begin using the basic Gnostic Psychic Attack-Breaking Ritual.

HOW TO USE THE BASIC GNOSTIC PSYCHIC ATTACK-BREAKING RITUAL

Up to this point, I have suggested that candles and incense are pretty much optional in the Gnostic Magical work, but as we get into breaking up psychic attack it is better to consider them mandatory. I would suggest two tapered candles, either white, blue or orange; a good sandalwood or protection incense; and a perfume oil (sandalwood, myhrr or uncrossing oil). Gather these along with a cup or glass of water in which you have dissolved about a tablespoon of salt. Then prepare the attack-breaking declaration by writing in your own hand on a piece of paper: "Through the fiery power of Marduk, Ra and Nergal, all negative or attacking spells or thoughtforms within the realm of my experience are reduced to worthless ashes. The watery power of Ishtar and Isis now rinses away the residue, leaving my aura and whole environment perfectly clean and conducive to my fresh and wonderful growth and progress. My new and successful way is guided by the insight of Thoth and Bast and nurtured by Osiris and Abraxas. As this paper burns, it is done. Thanks to all and so mote it be."

Before you sit down, sprinkle the area all around your altar with salt water (just dip your fingers into the cup and flick the water in an area about two to three feet all around your chair and altar). Then put the cup with the rest of the salt water in a safe place on your altar, sit down and light your candles and incense. Next use your finger to put a small amount of the perfume oil on your brow, throat and heart chakra areas. Now hold your written declaration between the palms of your hands as you picture yourself bathed in a shaft of bright white Light, then when you feel ready, read the declaration aloud with enjoyment and feeling four times. Just before you read it for the fifth time, touch the upper left-hand corner to your candle flame and read it just ahead of the flame, dropping it into the prepared receptacle as you finish.

Then as you sit quietly for a few moments, you should have a fresh, clean feeling. Give your spirit and energy transformer friends a few more moments of silence in case they have a message or bit of inspiration for you, then thank them all again, snuff your candles and go back to your normal routine. The first time you use this ritual, and any time you know you are under deliberate attack, repeat the ritual every day for at least five straight days—and longer if it feels necessary.

THE GNOSTIC PSYCHIC ATTACK-BREAKING RITUAL CAN SEEM TO BE A SOURCE OF GOOD LUCK

You may not feel the need to use this ritual, but I urge you to try it anyway; you may be quite pleasantly surprised, as this report from Harry S. shows us: "Al, I didn't feel that I was under any sort of attack, but I decided to try the psychic attack-breaking ritual on your recommendation. And I'm sure glad I did! My business has been quite steady for several years. I was doing well enough, but a strange thing happened. I did the ritual the first night and my next day's business was the best single day in our history! This was enough incentive to encourage me to keep it up for the five days you suggested. And it's so nice—business for the month we just completed is up almost 20% over what we've been averaging. And my

customers seem happier and nicer to us. Even my family
situation which I have felt was quite comfortable has been
especially loving and cooperative. I've tapered off to using the
ritual just once a week now. That seems to be enough to
maintain the happy new level of prosperity and cooperation.
Thanks much."

John G. was feeling very lonely and cut off from the
world. Let's let him tell us what happened: "I was miserable
and feeling mistreated on my job. I hadn't had anything in the
way of meaningful social activities in almost a year. My old
friends ignored me. Let's just say that my life was a mess. So it
didn't take much prodding to get me to try the Gnostic
Psychic Attack-Breaking Ritual. The second evening of the
ritual, a friend I hadn't seen in almost a year dropped in on me
and we had a wonderful visit. Next day I was invited to be an
alternate on a local political committee. The next day I was
notified that the insurance of my cars would drop from $700
to $300. Next day I attended the political meeting and was
invited to go to Washington, D.C. as an official representative
of the group (you might call it a paid lobbying trip). I had three
different dinner invitations from old friends during the week.
And suddenly everything on my job seems to be different. I'm
being treated with consideration and respect, and I'm told I'm
being groomed for promotion. These are just highlights of one
week from the time I started using the ritual. I can only say it
turned my life around from one of stark loneliness and misery
to one of happiness and a suddenly very bright looking future.
You can be sure that I will use the ritual at least once a week
for the rest of my life. It's wonderful."

And Janet B. wrote: "I had a pretty good idea that this one
friend of mine was into the black arts, but I didn't connect
that with my running string of bad luck and misfortunes until
I read one of your chapters on psychic attack. By this point my
husband and I had been fighting for weeks, but we were too
tired and weak to do much more than glare at each other. All
manner of bills for small accidents and broken doorknobs and
small appliances were accumulating, and even my cat was

sick—she ran up a $200 vet bill! Something had to give, so I was ready to admit the possibility of psychic attack and try the ritual. It's hard to explain the difference that resulted from that first usage, but I somehow felt cleaner inside than I had in a long while. My husband must have noticed the difference (I did the ritual in the late afternoon) because he actually smiled at me when he came home. We had a pleasant dinner for the first time in weeks, and he made love to me for the first time in about the same period. I did the ritual the next afternoon with considerably more zest and enthusiasm. This time my husband suggested that we go out to a local bingo party, and sure enough I won enough money to pay off all the messy little bills and the vet bill too! Words will never explain all of the difference. Even the house is nicer to me! I feel closets and cupboards seeming to want to cooperate where before I might have said I think this whole house hates me. I think I really understand what you mean about psychic ecology and keeping your aura clean now. I watch my feelings regularly and keep up the Gnostic cleansing work on a weekly basis—and we are happier and healthier now than we have ever been. Oh, yes, my husband also got a nice raise about a week ago. It was more than twice as much as we hoped for! Thanks to you and those wonderful energy transformer personalities."

THE GNOSTIC REVERSING RITUAL—FOR ELIMINATING CHRONIC OR EXTREMELY SEVERE SITUATIONS

Within the realm of the experience of all those with whom I have worked on these matters, I would say that something over 90% of the psychic problems are fully swept away by the Gnostic Psychic Attack-Breaking Ritual. This is another time where a clear conscience requires that you give the gentler approach a good chance to work for you. Thus the first bit of preparation for the Gnostic Reversing Ritual should be to use the Basic Gnostic Psychic Attack-Breaking Ritual for a full 22 consecutive days. Then if you still need the reversing ritual you can do it without guilt or reservation, simply claiming the peace and good that are certainly your own.

When you decide that the reversing ritual is necessary, stop by your local five-and-ten-cent store or the notions section of a department store and pick up a small, inexpensive hand mirror. Write your initials on a small, circular piece of paper (one inch or less in diameter) and glue the paper on the center of the reflecting side of the mirror (with your initials facing out so you can read them). You will use the same candles, incense, salt water and perfume oil as for the psychic attack-breaking ritual, so all that remains in the way of preparation is to handwrite the reversing declaration on a separate piece of paper. It should read: "By the power of Osiris, Ishtar, Nergal, Marduk and Bast, all attacking spells and thoughtforms must hit this mirror instead of me. They are then reflected with full force to neutralize the source of attack that it may harm me no more. I seek not revenge nor to hurt another, simply to positively assert my right to live a healthy, peaceful, loving and prosperous life without outside inter-ference of any kind. From this day forward, all spells and attacks against me are reversed *now and forevermore*. My loving thanks to all. So mote it be."

Take all of your materials to your altar area now and you will be ready to perform the reversing ritual.

HOW TO PERFORM THE GNOSTIC REVERSING RITUAL TO RID YOURSELF OF EVEN THE STRONGEST PSYCHIC ATTACK

Open the ritual by sprinkling the salt water, lighting your candles and incense and anointing your brow, throat and heart chakras with perfume oil—just as you have been doing to start the attack-breaking ritual. When you are ready, place your declaration face down on the shiny side of the mirror, then pick them up together and hold them between the palms of your hands as you picture yourself bathed in a shaft of bright white Light. *Will* a good flow of energy between your hands and say: "The mirror, declaration and I are now linked together as one, ready to work permanently as a powerfully positive unit."

Put the declaration down safely within reach, and lay the mirror face up near the center of your altar. With a fingertip full of perfume oil, trace the outline of a circle around the outer edge of the small paper with your initials on the center of the mirror and state: "This powerful oil protects me now as the mirror is ready to do its good work." Then pick up your declaration and read it aloud clearly and with feeling four times. Just before the fifth reading, touch the upper left-hand corner of the paper to your candle flame and complete your reading just ahead of the flame, dropping the paper into the prepared receptacle as before.

Again sit quietly in case your spirit friends want to reach you with special instructions or inspiration. And when you feel ready, thank them all once more, snuff your candles and go back to your normal routine. However, it is probably a very good idea to follow up on this ritual with the cleansing power of the Gnostic Psychic Attack-Breaking Ritual, if for no other reason than just to sweep away any psychic residue. If you feel it necessary to repeat the reversing ritual, by all means do so. But again if you fail to achieve significant results within 22 days of regularly using the reversing ritual, I suggest that you write me for specific advice. (My address is given at the end of the last chapter of this book.)

Charlie H. is a manufacturer's representative and occasionally a materials broker. His use of the ritual will help you understand its effectiveness. Here is his report: "I knew I was in a slump, but try as I might I hadn't been able to break it. My normal income had averaged between fifty and eighty thousand a year for quite a few years on commissions ranging from a few hundred to four or five thousand dollars on individual deals. But it seemed as though the bottom had dropped out of things. For three months in a row I had scratched and sweated and had not quite been able to cover my overhead, much less add something to my own net income! Finally I realized that that fascinating woman I had reluctantly turned down because I'm a happily married man had done more than just curse me to my face. The psychic attack ritual had helped a little. During those 22 days I estimate I netted a thousand or so, but it was still WAY below par, and I knew that I had to go on to the reversing ritual. So I acquired the mirror, wrote out the declaration in due course and prepared to do the biggie. Things were still not much better, so I felt OK, let's do it! The morning of the day after I did the reversing ritual I got a phone call. It involved about two solid hours on the telephone to various of my contacts, but the commission I earned was just over one hundred thousand dollars! Thanks, Al, for giving us the ammunition to win. Life is indeed comfortable again."

Helen D. had this to report: "I am still in debt to the doctors, but things are looking up now. For almost three years I suffered with terrible pains in my back and legs. I went to specialist after specialist, but no one could find a cause for the pain and the pain pills they gave me never really helped much either. I was sure I was about to become addicted to something, and even considered suicide as the only way to escape the excruciating pain. Then I realized that there must be a psychic rather than a physical cause. So I started with the Gnostic Psychic Attack-Breaking Ritual, and after the first usage I got wonderful relief. I was elated, but the relief only lasted about an hour, then the pain came back. For a week I did that ritual morning and evening and got about an hour's solace each time. Then I decided that 22 days was too long to wait. I used the reversing ritual on the evening of the eighth day AND SLEPT ALL NIGHT for the first time in three years! I awoke with some pain, so repeated the reversing ritual right after breakfast, and had quite a good day.

"To summarize, I have done the reversing twice a day for 15 days, and for the last week I have been PAIN FREE! I plan to slack it off to once a day now, and in a reasonable time hopefully to once a week. Al, you'll never know the feeling of relief and gratitude in my heart. Thanks to you for introducing me to the wonderful energy transformer personalities and the magnificent Gnostic Magic that comes with them. Life is pleasant again, and I'm about to turn my new-found magical talents to manifesting the money to pay off those doctor bills. In passing, I want to tell you that a close cousin developed the same symptoms I got rid of just about the time of my release. I did know that she had been very jealous of me, but never thought she would have stooped to sending me such a curse. It seems to have gone back to her, but I cannot feel guilty or even sorry for her. That part is quite properly between her and the forces she invoked to make me suffer. Again my thanks to all."

HOW TO GET QUICK AND EASY PROTECTION FROM OTHER PEOPLE'S TENSIONS AND PRESSURE

We all have those times when we know we have to go into the company of people who are excessively tense or who will try to put psychological pressure on us. In giving you this quickie remedy, I also have the opportunity to introduce another facet of Gnostic Magic which will prove quite invaluable in the more powerful work to come. Although the written history of the Gnostics is quite sketchy, we do know that they put much stock in the psychic and magical power of gemstones. Since I have been into Gnostic Magic for a number of years, you will find a rather comprehensive discussion of the power of gemstones in both my *Miracle Spiritology* and *Magic of New Ishtar Power*. Rather than repeat that part of the work, I will bring in selected stones for special applications throughout the rest of this book.

Now let's consider handling tension and pressure. Your solar plexus chakra is always the first point of your beingness that is attacked by the presence of others who are tense or by those who are applying pressure to you. To protect this one chakra is to ward off at least 90% of the attacking energy. If you are caught unprepared in a super tense situation, you should develop a reflex action whereby you cover your solar plexus with your hand (either is OK, but the left is preferable for a right-handed person). On the other hand, you would look a bit silly walking around very long with a hand obviously covering your stomach/waist area. Thus we find that there are cosmetic as well as psychic reasons for resorting to a bit of gemstone help.

There is an inexpensive gemstone called tiger eye that is ideally suited to this task, and it is quite simple to use. Before you head into a known area of tension, simply tape a nice tiger eye stone to your solar plexus area. Some people use regular transparent tape, but I am more comfortable using the sheer surgical tape that is readily available at your local super market or drug store. For a touch of added power, take the stone to your altar and do the psychic attack-breaking ritual. At the end of the ritual, hold the stone up in your hand and ask that it be especially charged with protective power for you. Then tape it in place and head out to meet the world with the knowledge that its tensions cannot get through the stone to affect you. This, with one of our basic effectiveness rituals, can make you a very comfortable winner.

John K's report may help you to understand: "I am a salesman in a highly competitive field. I have always done well at getting my share of business, but the tensions are real man killers. You constantly deal with people who are insecure and afraid to make decisions, and it's only natural that the tension level by the end of the day requires a whole pitcher of martinis before you can unwind enough to eat. Then you suggested that I try a tiger eye. It was a major investment; I paid all of three dollars for a nice size stone. I did the psychic attack-breaking ritual that evening mostly by way of con-secrating the stone, and taped it to my solar plexus before setting out for my next day's work. I had already been using the Ishtar/Abraxas effectiveness ritual, and this was really the capper. I came home after a highly successful day quite relaxed and at peace. Yes, I had a martini before dinner, but only ONE! I enjoyed the evening as I had not for a long time. The bottom line is my sales are comfortably up, my blood pressure is down, I come home relaxed in the evening, and I'm told that I have become something of a fair-haired boy about the company. I am being pointed out as an example of success to new salesmen, and there are very nice rumors of my impending promotion to regional sales manager. And the best part is, I KNOW that I can handle it now. My special thanks to you all."

GNOSTIC MAGIC MIND JOGGERS

1. YOU are undoubtedly subjected to some degree of psychic attack virtually every day.
2. Most psychic attack is not deliberate, but like being shot, the result is the same whether or not it was deliberate.
3. Have a good look at the suggested symptoms of psychic attack; we don't want to become paranoid, but it is wise to be concerned with your overall psychic ecology.
4. The Basic Gnostic Psychic Attack-Breaking Ritual is a gentle and safe way of cleansing your aura and surroundings to sweep away any accumulations of negative or attacking psychic energy.
5. The immediate result of using the attack-breaking ritual should be a fresh, clean feeling. You will know you have done it well as the symptoms of attack fade away to nothing.
6. The Gnostic Attack-Breaking Ritual will often seem to be a source of good luck. Do use it regularly whether you feel you need it or not.
7. The Gnostic Reversing Ritual should sweep away any attack not removed by the attack-breaking ritual. Use this one sparingly, and preferably only after 22 straight days of the attack-breaking ritual.
8. A tiger eye (gemstone) is an excellent source of extra protection from tension. Tape one to your solar plexus before you go into places of tension, and sail through with ease and comfort.

8

How Gnostic Magic Rites Free You or a Loved One from Obsessing or Possessing Entities — or Bad Habits

Over the last decade or more, movies like *The Exorcist*, *Rosemary's Baby*, *The Omen* and many others have dramatized and overstated the negative side of the occult. We have no reason to emphasize the bizzare here, but it is necessary to recognize that there may be times when a negative person passes through the grave into the spirit world and remains in a sort of earthbound state in order to seek revenge or in some other way to fulfill a burning unfinished desire by borrowing your physical body. There are other possibilities and reasons too, and we will seek to unfold them as necessary along the way. But right here I want to stress that there are also purely positive applications for the exorcism process, such as breaking bad habits and improving your psychic ecology. So even if you never expect to do battle with an entity for the control of your own body or to free a loved one, you will find that there is still much of use to you in this chapter. If you are impatient to get on to something else, it's OK to skip ahead, but promise yourself to come back and master the work of this chapter in order to become a fully rounded and powerful Gnostic Magician.

RECOGNIZING THE DIFFERENCE BETWEEN
YOU AND THE HABIT OR ENTITY

In our last two chapters we were concerned with recognizing the controlling suggestions, actions and thoughtforms of others. Now let's look at the other things that "run" you or control you, but that have still hidden behind the disguise of "myself." If you have ever been a fairly heavy cigarette smoker, for instance, it is easy to remember that a substantial part of the habit is or was on the subliminal or preconscious level. If you are a man, the pack sits in your shirt pocket and it is virtually a reflex action for your hand to take a cigarette and light it while the conscious part of you is reading, working or even carrying on a conversation. Thus in effect the habit has become a living entity which fulfills its own desires without the full consent of your conscious mind. Alcoholism and some addictive drugs may form even more powerful living entities, but the principle is the same. And indeed the principle of control (obsession or possession) of your body by any entity external to yourself takes place through exactly the same mechanism.

A brief examination of the mechanism itself will give us a new set of tools with which to protect ourselves and eliminate those actions that are not to our enlightened best interest. The body of an entity is made of the same emotional energy as your own astral (or emotional) body. An entity which used to inhabit a human physical body is of course a much more complex organism than the entity of a habit such as smoking, but its method of causing you to accede to its will is the same. The entity focuses on its desire and literally bombards the right sections of your astral beingness with these desire vibrations. Sometimes the physical body will simply act on this as if the desire were that of its own astral body, or if the impulse reaches the conscious level it is misinterpreted as "*I* want this." And if there are no compelling reasons against it already known to your mind, you will proceed to gratify the desire of the entity just as if it were your own desire. Thus we see that the final trick in gaining complete control of your organism is to recognize the difference—in effect to mentally and emotionally separate *you* and your own desires from the entity and its desires.

In a very real sense, then, the classic line of Flip Wilson's, "The devil made me do it," may be substantially correct—but it is still YOU who suffers the consequences of the action, not the entity or "devil"! But a good working understanding of the mechanism will give you the tools and determination to win, where otherwise you might drift along, being controlled by any old set of entities or habits, for the rest of your life.

HOW TO DECIDE THAT YOU NEED TO PRACTICE EXORCISM

Let's begin by saying that nothing in the preceding section was intended to suggest that you give up all of life's pleasures. On the habit level, I myself did quit cigarette smoking a few years ago because it always irritated my throat, but I still smoke a pipe and an occasional cigar, and I enjoy a few drinks as well as the next guy. Any of these things done for real enjoyment and in moderation are neither bad for you nor should they be considered obsessing entities. But it is a good idea to take a searching look at yourself at least once a month to see the direction of your progress and check for negative trends and influences. When you note something that is not to your liking, immediately set it aside in your thinking as something that is NOT you. This step alone will eliminate many minor habits and trends before they have a chance to grow into full-fledged entities. But for those that don't leave by your invitation, the exorcism process is indeed indicated.

And finally, the Gnostic Exorcism Rite is pleasant and quite safe. So just as in our last chapter I felt it proper to say, "When in doubt, use the Gnostic Psychic Attack-Breaking Ritual," here I feel it equally proper to say, "When in doubt USE the Gnostic Exorcism Rite." Again the preparation should include gathering candles, sandalwood or exorcism incense, sandalwood or exorcism perfume oil, and a cup of salt water. Then prepare the exorcism declaration by writing in your own hand, "I joyously accept the help of Nergal and Osiris in restraining all obsessive or possessive entities and thoughtforms around me. They are joined by Ra and Ishtar who provide instructions on the way it is proper for entities and thoughtforms to act and grow. Marduk now burns away any of their remaining negativity, and they are led by Thoth and Bast to the place of their own highest good, away from me and able to cause no further disruptions in my life. As this paper burns, the exorcism is complete. I give thanks for my own wonderful freedom and for the help in leading the formerly negative beings to their place of Light and growth. So mote it be." And sign it with your normal signature.

One optional but very powerful extra bit of preparation would be to perform the Ritual of Joy just before you start your Gnostic Exorcism Rite. This will strengthen your ties to the energy transformer personalities and set the mood of good will to insure that there will be no negative manifestations during the exorcism itself.

USING THE GNOSTIC EXORCISM RITE FOR YOURSELF

To begin the rite, sprinkle the area around your altar liberally with the salt water, then put the cup with some of the salt water still in it in a safe place on your altar. Light your candles and incense, and anoint your brow, throat and heart chakras with the perfume oil. Then speak aloud, "Good friends, Isis, Nergal, Ra, Ishtar, Osiris, Marduk, Thoth, Bast and Abraxas, I greet you in love and good fellowship and invite your further help in my growth and progress. I seek my rightful total freedom from the influence and control of other entities or thoughtforms. I approach the task in good will, seeking truly the highest good for us all, and I know that with your invincible help it is done now."

Next, hold your exorcism declaration between the palms of your hands as you picture yourself bathed in bright white Light. When you feel ready, begin reading the declaration aloud while vividly picturing the process: see the gentle but firm restraint of the beings by Nergal and Osiris, feel the instruction being given by Ra and Ishtar, see the purifying electric blue energy of Marduk actually reprogramming the beings as may be necessary, and watch them being gently but firmly led away by Thoth and Bast. Repeat the reading of the declaration until you feel fresh and clean and completely free of entity or thoughtform interference, or at least until you have done four full readings. Then touch the upper left-hand corner of the paper to your candle flame and read it once more just ahead of the flame. Drop the residue into the receptacle at the end as always. Then sit quietly to see what inspiration or instruction may come to you from the energy transformer personalities or your spirit people. When you are ready, thank all your friends once more, snuff your candles and go back to your normal routine.

RESULTS FROM USING THE GNOSTIC EXORCISM RITE

Mary H. was a widow for 15 years before she found the help she needed. Here is her report: "I was married at 16 to a person whom I came to know as the meanest man in the world. For 20 years he ridiculed me in public and tormented me in all possible ways. Every time I tried to leave he caught me, brought me back and beat me up. Then he died and I honestly rejoiced! But my happiness was extremely short lived. Two days after the funeral he showed up in spirit form and started to torment me all over again. I won't bore you with the details, but every time I got a man friend, the malevolent spirit of my dead husband would spook him so badly I never saw him again. This being woke me many times each night by biting me somewhere—so hard you could actually see the teeth marks the next morning! The taunting was continuous and quite unbearable. Naturally I tried my church, mediums and even gypsies, but nobody was able to help me. He even scared a medical doctor so badly that he ran from my house shaking with fear!

"When I looked over the Gnostic Exorcism Rite, I almost didn't bother to try. The gently but firmly bit didn't appear to have a chance on that ornery so and so; but that's all there was at hand and you know I was desperate, so I tried it. I'm sure glad I took your suggestion to use the joy ritual first. He was there heckling during that part, but it set a good mood for me with the energy transformer personalities. I could actually hear the sounds of struggling in the room as I got well into the ritual. At about the fourth reading of the declaration he began to plead with me, 'Please don't let them take me away from you; I'll be lost without you,' so I kept on with renewed enthusiasm. After about ten readings, things had pretty well calmed down, but I wanted to be sure so I kept it up. It was probably about the twenty-first time that I touched the paper to my candle and completed the rite. It was a complete success! I know that he is much better off where they took him, and I'm sort of a 51-year-old teenager. I'm dating four men and having a ball while carefully getting ready for a truly happy marriage. Al, I KNOW it's *my turn* ! Thanks to all—and it's so wonderful to realize that I know what to do if I ever get into that kind of trouble again."

Charlie B. had a completely different problem. Let's let him tell us how he handled it: "When I was a teenager it was fashionable to be a heavy smoker. I started seriously at 16 and smoked two or more packs of cigarettes a day for about 30 years. A few years ago, what with all the bad press about heavy smoking, I decided it would be a good idea to quit. Man, I tried everything—all kinds of filters, the professional non-smoking programs, cold turkey, and you name it—but NOTHING worked. You might say I realized I was hooked. Then I got into your Gnostic Magic. The idea of separating the habit from myself made sense, and I did see how completely independent of me it really was. But that was clearly not enough to make such a well-established thoughtform go away, so the exorcism rite was necessary. I did the exorcism rite at bedtime and actually made it until about noon the next day before I just had to have a cigarette. I made it through the rest of the day on slightly less than one pack, and that in itself was impressive. So I repeated the exorcism that night, and made it clear to 3:00 P.M. before it got to me. It took just about three weeks of repeating the exorcism rite each night at bedtime to be sure I'm rid of it. Now on those rare occasions when someone's smoking smells good to me (most often it smells horrible—I'm told that nothing is so complaining as a newly reformed smoker), I just laugh and say, 'you're not going to hook me again,' and even the hint of the desire is gone. There was slight weight problem at first because everything tasted so much better, but I handled that with two new exorcism sessions and all is beautiful!"

Bob L. used it this way: "When I got to thinking about separating you from your bad habit or obsession I weighed 360 pounds and my friends called me by the obvious nickname, 'the Blimp.' I guess I didn't realize how much I was missing until I found out that my wife had a boyfriend on the side. I decided to launch a crash program to return to a truly normal life. Since I wasn't quite sure what to do, I began using the Gnostic Blockbuster Limitation-Breaking Ritual, the Gnostic Psychic Attack-Breaking Ritual, and the Gnostic Exorcism Rite. I figured that by hitting it from three sides simultaneously I ought to get some good results. Al, I've always had an appetite like a man of 400 to 500 pounds, but almost overnight I found myself relishing low calorie salads and just barely picking at the meat and potatoes. I get plenty of exercise anyway, so the pounds literally started peeling off. I shed about 30 pounds the first month, and 25 each the next two months. After the first few weeks when I saw it was really working, I slacked off to doing the three rituals in rotation, one each night. The fourth, fifth and sixth months I continued to lose at a rate of about 20 pounds a month. By this point I was beginning to look pretty good in my mirror. I have finally leveled off my weight at 180 pounds, which looks just right for my build.

"The story might be better if I could tell you this saved my marriage. It didn't—she ran off with the other guy—but that made for a very inexpensive divorce and suddenly I find myself quite a center of popularity with the ladies. Now I watch my weight almost daily, and if it starts to creep up at all, I go right back to my three rituals. I never quite figured out which one did the trick, and why take chances? For happy fall-out, obviously I feel better and am enjoying a wonderfully varied love life. I have been moved out of the shop into an executive position (I found out that it was only my appearance that had held me back for several years), so I'm making lots more money. Most of all I really enjoy life again."

HOW TO FREE A LOVED ONE FROM OBSESSIONS OR BAD HABITS

Another advantage of learning to separate yourself from your shortcomings and bad habits is that it becomes easy to extend the same consideration to your friends and loved ones. Where you make the mental separation and can talk it over with the other person, you may be able to get him or her to join you in doing the exorcism rite together. This is a very powerful approach, since you will learn that two working together are at least as powerful as four working independently. If you get a negative response, or if you know you would, all is still not lost. You can do the ritual for him or her. Sometimes the person may be so fully controlled by the entity or habit any discussion is impossible, but it is always well to keep in mind that it is NOT your purpose to substitute YOUR control for that of the entity or habit. Stay pure and work ONLY for the person's freedom from obsession and control— otherwise someone else may have to do him or her a ritual to get rid of your controlling influence.

In addition to the normal preparations for the exorcism rite, you will need something to be a stand-in or to take the place of the person you wish to help. A photograph or snapshot of the person (particularly if you can get one taken when he or she was in a happy mood or time of life) is best, but a handwritten note or signature is almost as strong a tie. Lacking both of these, any article that has belonged to the person is helpful, but if you have nothing tangible at all you can still use your own clear *mental* picture of the person and do quite well for him or her.

This time the exorcism declaration should read: "As [*insert the name of the person to be helped*], I joyously accept the help of Nergal and Osiris ... [*then everything stays the same until we reach this next part* ...] ... the exorcism is complete. I give thanks for [*insert the name again*]'s wonderful freedom and for the help in leading the formerly negative beings to their place of Light and growth. So mote it be." (Then sign it, the person's name by your name.[1]

PERFORMING THE GNOSTIC EXORCISM RITE
FOR ANOTHER PERSON

In working for another person it is all the more important to begin with the ritual of joy to be sure you have established a mood of good will and confidence along with a strong set of ties to the energy transformer personalities. Open the exorcism rite itself with the salt water, candles, incense and perfume oil just as if you were going to do it for yourself. Then if you have a tangible tie to the patient (picture, letter, article), also anoint it with your perfume oil.

As you now hold the exorcism declaration between your palms, picture yourself *and* the patient bathed in bright white Light. Pick up the tangible article if you have one and hold it next to the declaration as you state aloud: "By the power of attunement through this [picture, letter, etc., or "By the power of attunement through my strong mental picture"], and the loving power of the white Light, I make this declaration for and AS...." *(State the person's name.)*

Then speak aloud: "Good friends, Isis, Nergal, Ra, Ishtar, Osiris, Marduk, Thoth, Bast and Abraxas, I greet you in love and good fellowship and invite your further help in the growth and progress of [*the patient's name*]. I seek his (or her) rightful total freedom from the influence and control of other entities or thoughtforms. I approach the task in good will, seeking truly the highest good for us all, and I know that with your invincible help it is done now."

When you are ready, read the exorcism declaration at least four times before touching it to your candle flame for the final reading. Picture the negatives restrained and purified with each reading. At the conslusion, sit quietly to see if there are any further instructions from your spirit people or the energy transformer personalities as to other ways you should help the person. When it feels finished, thank all your good friends again, snuff your candles and go back to your normal routine.

George R. had occasion to use the exorcism rite for his wife, as this report will explain: "It took a long time to come to the realization that my wife was an alcoholic. She has always been a lovely, lovable lady and this made it hurt all the more to see her ruining her health as well as our social position with her excessive drinking. I tried to get her into Alcoholics Anonymous, but it didn't work because she refused to accept the fact that she had a drinking problem. I'll admit to considering divorce because it was all such a mess, but fortunately I got to thinking about the Gnostic ideas I got from you and it became quite easy to separate the drinking problem from my lovely wife. And since I could get no cooperation, the only choice was to treat it as an obsessing entity and treat her for its removal without her cooperation or knowledge. I took one of our wedding pictures for a positive point of contact because I knew she was happy and not an excessive drinker at that time. I added one word to the exorcism declaration to make it feel more specific to me. So it began, 'I joyously accept the help of Nergal and Osiris in restraining all obsessive or possessive entities and *drinking* thoughtforms around Gloria. ... ' I kept thinking how happy we were on our honeymoon all through the ritual of joy and the other preparations, and the visualization of the energy transformer personalities reworking the entities and thoughtforms was a special kind of joy to me. I'd like to tell you that I won it in just one night, but that's not the way it happened.

"As a matter of fact, there was a bit of a negative reaction on the first night. I came back into the den where my wife was drinking and she (or I would say the entity) threw a vase at me! But I took that as encouragement that I was getting through to the entity and resolved to do it daily until I attained total victory. It seemed sort of nip and tuck for the first week, but something inside me told me that perseverance could win, so I stuck with it. The result is better than I dared hope. It wasn't a complete cessation of her drinking; she just suddenly passed a rule for herself that one drink before dinner and two after would be her absolute limit. I'm so proud of her! We've been in social situations where the pressure and temptation to go way over her limit was certainly present, but she invariably sticks by her guns. It has been two full months since she passed her rule and she has not violated it even once! I still do the exorcism for her (secretly) about once a week just for safety, but it's all so wonderful, I have my loving and lovely wife back whole and real. My thanks go out to all every day."

Marilyn H. used it this way: "My early teenage son changed almost overnight from a bright and friendly A student to a surly would-be drop-out. All communication was gone; it seemed that there was just no way I could reach him. Clearly this was not my son, so there was no question about using the Gnostic Exorcism Rite. I took a picture from a happy recent vacation for my point of contact, gathered my supplies and headed for my altar. During the ritual of joy, I got a bit of instruction. They told me I was a bit too tense about this so I should get a tiger eye for my solar plexus and a piece of carnelian for my spleen center. I took the advice and went to my local lapidary before starting the exorcism rite. And that was good advice; I could feel the difference in me as I started to work. Without those stones I know that I would have been too tense and serious to get the full cooperation of the energy transformer personalities. But this was a good show. Oh, how I enjoyed picturing those entities being handled! I feasted on this and repeated the declaration for probably 15 to 20 times before I felt ready to complete the rite by burning the piece of paper. Afterward I felt very good, and my son came home that evening quite his old self. I've decided to do the exorcism for him at least twice a month for safety, but it's wonderful to see him diving into his educational processes again. I think we got it in time to save his grades for the semester. A special thanks to all!''

GNOSTIC MAGIC MIND JOGGERS

1. The possibility of entity obsession is real enough, but bad habits function in the same way, so the exorcism work is useful in eliminating either or both problems.
2. The trick to understanding the need for exorcism is to separate the negative actions or desires from you. See them as an external force seeking its gratification by controlling your emotions and body.
3. If the act of making the mental separation doesn't eliminate the problem, then the Gnostic Exorcism Rite is indicated.
4. It is best to use the ritual of joy in preparation for the exorcism work to establish a firm tie to your helpful energy transformer personalities so the work can be done with pleasure and good fellowship.
5. Results from the Gnostic Exorcism Rite will be positive and good. When in doubt, USE IT.
6. When a friend or loved one is acting negatively or irrationally, separate the actions from the person mentally just as you would for yourself.
7. With that approach, if you can't talk the person out of the actions, try to get him or her to do the exorcism rite with you.
8. Even without the knowledge or cooperation of the patient, you can do a successful exorcism for him or her. Take care that you don't try to establish a control of your own over the person, but use the rite in good faith and WIN. You will help the person and all who associate with him or her.

9

Attract and Hold the Interest and Loyalty of Your Perfect Lover with Gnostic Magic Rites

In Chapter 5, the love and friendship chapter, we introduced a basic set of Gnostic fundamentals that generally prove enough by themselves to bring magnificent changes in your love life. But if you are still waiting to find your wonderful lover and mate, or if you find that your present love relationship is still a bit frayed around the edges, we have plenty of fresh help for you in the work of this chapter. If everything is fine for you in this department and you want to skip ahead to something that seems more pressing to you, that's OK, but promise yourself that you will come back and master this work because it contains a positive entity-building process that we will use in later, deeper parts of the Gnostic Magical lore.

THE GNOSTIC MAGICIAN'S FIRST QUESTION—WHAT DO YOU HAVE TO GIVE?

Since the classic Gnostic definition of love is *givingness*, it is logical that the first part of attracting a wonderful mate is to give thought to what you have to give to a relationship. This also helps you to disassociate your thinking from the "I need and I want" syndrome to the givingness that is more practical to work with. After all, attracting a mate is something of an advertising project and the beginning of good advertising is an in-depth assessment of the product, with hopefully a good shot at packaging design. In our last chapter we learned how to get rid of entities, so in this one we will know it is safe to create an entity of your own whose only reason for existing is to attract your mate, then stay close to keep the relationship exciting and alive. But no matter how good a "salesman" we help you create, its effectiveness will be hindered or greatly helped by the quality of the package you give it to "market" for you.

This is a good time for what I like to call a *mirror exercise*. Put yourself in the mood of an amateur ad man, and settle down comfortably with pencil and paper in front of your mirror to have a good look at the product you are undertaking to market. Start with the external appearance; first note the obvious strong points and write them down. Next make notes of little things that can be done easily to improve the physical appearance of the package. What can be done to make this package look more wholesome? More erotic? More appealing? And more practical? Now how would you describe this person's occupation? Can you make your description sound a lot more positive? More glamorous? More stable? How would you describe this person's sense of humor? Personality? Spirituality? Especially appealing features?

Keep your list of notes as brief as possible, but focus on getting real quality into this section of the work. The idea is to put your very best foot forward, and it is your intimate knowledge of your subject that is our greatest asset in getting prepared to WIN. Spend as much time and as many sessions as necessary to know that you have done a good job on it. We will make this a very powerful tool for you in just a few moments, but first let's get to the other tools you will need for the GNOSTIC LOVER-ATTRACTING RITUAL.

COMPLETING YOUR PREPARATIONS FOR THE GNOSTIC LOVER-ATTRACTING RITUAL

The physical list, or at least the feeling of what you really have to give, is the most important part of the preparation, but there are several more things you should gather to make your ritual super powerful and effective. In the old Gnostic times the lodestone was highly prized for its magnetic qualities. Today we have many magnets that are stronger, but the untreated natural state of a small piece of lodestone has a magical power all its own. If you can't find a piece of lodestone, you can do almost as well with a small magnet such as you might find sewn into a potholder. Your lodestone or magnet plus a small picture or snapshot of yourself should go to your altar area along with tapered red, pink or green candles, frankincense or love oil, frankincense or love incense and a glass or cup of salt water. This plus the regular goodies for the Gnostic Ritual of Joy completes the physical preparations.

But before you start, we need a brief discussion of the idea of creating your own living entity. Many people unconsciously create such entities, all too often with negative emotional energy. The old metaphysical tradition teaches that *thoughts are things* , but the terminology is slightly in error. A thought by itself is nothing, but strong feelings focused on a thought do create a "thing," a living entity of emotional energy which strives to fulfill the thought until it is either completely exhausted or it accomplishes its purpose. Thus we can readily understand the "thoughts are things" idea: the metaphysician teaches us to think only positive thoughts, so if we do get emotion in them to create an entity it will be a friendly one, bent on doing good.

Here the Gnostic Magician has an advantage. He clearly understands the creative process and carefully focuses his most powerful emotional energies on his chosen idea, and the results become quite consistent, without the many stillborn creations you may have begotten in the past. Picture the entity creation process clearly now and take this understanding to your well-prepared altar and we will create your lover-attracting entity easily and enjoyably.

HOW TO USE THE GNOSTIC LOVER-ATTRACTING RITUAL

Begin the ritual by sprinkling salt water all around your altar area, then put the cup with the remaining salt water on your altar. Sit down, light your candles and incense and anoint your brow, throat and heart chakras with your oil. Then have a really enjoyable ritual of joy. The length of time here is quite varied, just enough to produce a very good mood and the feeling of solid and happy contact with the energy transformer personalities. When you are ready for the lover-attracting part, begin by placing your picture (face up with the head facing north) on your altar and putting the lodestone (or magnet) on the area of the picture that includes your heart. (Note: if you are using a magnet rather than the lodestone, see that the north-seeking pole is facing north.) Then announce aloud: "Beloved teachers and energy transformer personalities, I ask your wonderful help in building an entity programmed to attract my perfect lover. I have placed this bit of magnetic material on my picture to form the nucleus of attraction and serve as a focal point for the energies of creation and attraction. I invite you to join in the good fellowship of creating together."

Now hold your hands about six inches apart with the palms facing in around your picture and lodestone. It's OK to rest the edges of your hands on the surface of your altar to keep your arms from getting tired. Picture a flow of bright red energy from your root center focusing between your palms and speak, "Dear Nergal, with your help I put the energy of life, power and sexual attraction into this new entity." Now picture the flow of bright orange energy from your spleen center and say, "Mighty Ra, with your help I put the faculties of intelligence and good judgment into the entity"; then picture the yellow from your solar plexus and say, "Brother Ishtar, with your help I endow the entity with intuition and effectiveness." Continue by sending the green energy from your heart chakra, saying, "Good Osiris, with your help I fill this entity with love, strength and courage"; then the electric blue from your throat chakra, saying, "Brother Marduk, with your help I give the entity creativity and the power to break up negative conditions"; then add the indigo energy from your brow center, saying, "Wise Thoth, with your help I endow the entity with wisdom, versatility and the power of excellent communications"; then the violet energy from your crown chakra, saying, "Lovely Bast, with your help I fill the entity with spirituality and spiritual power."

You are now ready to program your well-balanced entity to do its good work for you. Continue by saying, "Wonderful Isis and Abraxas, with your help I now program this entity to find and bring to me my perfect lover, then stay with us to keep the relationship happy and alive." Then return in thought to your list of good qualities, and speak or think them into the entity with the idea that it will seek out the person who will most appreciate you, while being available and fully able to bring equivalent good to a well-balanced, practical and totally fulfilling relationship. Talk to the entity as you would to a salesman who is about to set out to market your product, and enjoy getting him all fired up with enthusiasm.

Finally, instruct the entity as to the times of day that you will return to your altar for communication and mutual encouragement. Then sit quietly for a few moments to see if there is guidance for you from the new entity or from your friends in spirit, and when you are ready, give your warmest thanks to all. Know that it is done, snuff your candles and go back to your normal routine.

Do make a careful mental note about the location of the entity-building process here in this chapter. Obviously we can use entities for other things also. You will find this a tremendously powerful tool as we go deeper into the Gnostic Magical lore in the rest of this book.

RESULTS FROM THE GNOSTIC LOVER-ATTRACTING RITUAL

We have files full of fun feedback on this ritual, so much so that it was hard to make a choice. Let's look at this one from Sally D.: "I was quite lonely when I used the lover-attracting ritual, and had literally no prospects. It was fun to feel that I was building an entity all my own, but at first I was afraid I hadn't done it right. I did the ritual on a Tuesday, and sat to talk to my entity each night. Nothing at all happened until Saturday evening, when at my altar I got a very strong urge to attend church the next morning. This was out of the ordinary because it had been at least six months since I had been inside a church. It seemed to be direction from my entity, so I decided to cooperate. And it was wonderful! I bumped into some old friends who asked me to stop at their house after church to meet a friend of theirs. There was a feeling of quiet enthusiasm around me (yes, from my entity), so I accepted. He turned out to be the man of my dreams, and it was mutual. We had a glorious five-week courtship before we decided to get married. And you might say we're still newlyweds, but we both know that this one is for keeps. It's wonderful!"

John R. reported: "The nature of my work pretty well keep me from meeting nice girls that way, and I don't like the idea of singles' bars, so I was in a quandary. I did the lover-attracting ritual almost tongue in cheek, but I'll admit I had a good time at it. And it was just the next afternoon that I was in my car about to pull out into the traffic when the car in front of me suddenly backed up right into me. We both got out to look at the potential damage, and joyfully there was none. But it was something like the storybook idea of love at first sight. I asked for her name and phone number 'in case there was latent damage,' but we both knew why I really wanted it. I called her that evening and invited her on a dinner date. She accepted without hesitation, and it was one of those dream situations. We share so many interests and have so much in common it's almost eerie. We're living together very happily with the mutual promise that we'll marry within a year. She wanted to be really sure, and I go along without hesitation. We were literally made for each other and all will be well for many, many years."

And Irene N. reported her results this way: "I was widowed at 63 and for three years I learned the meaning of the statistics which say that an older woman has very little chance of finding a suitable new mate. My love life looked hopeless indeed, so my decision to try the Gnostic Lover-Attracting Ritual was more for the fun and magic of it than with any real expectation of results. There was a special thrill to feeling I had created my entity—not all that different from motherhood. So it was fun to meet with and nourish my 'child' each evening. There was a real feeling of companionship from the entity which I enjoyed. About the eleventh evening of this I seemed to sense a special kind of excitement from the entity. And only a few minutes later my phone rang. It was a friend saying she had just met a very old friend of mine, and asking if it was all right to drop over. Of course I said yes, and was it a surprise! The old friend turned out to be literally the boy next door from my childhood. Years ago we had vowed to meet and marry when my family moved us away—I guess I was 13 at the time. We had been pretty much out of touch, our last exchange of letters being when I got married at 19, but it was almost as if we had never been separated! We were both alone, and now we picked up the old relationship, but with the appreciation of experience. In spite of the social security problems we decided we're still 'square' enough to want to be married. The wedding is next week! Magnificent!"

THE GNOSTIC LOVE RENEWAL RITE

Perhaps more of us tend to need to renew or refurbish a slipping love affair or simply to pump fresh life into an aging marriage rather than attract a new mate. So this section should be studied well. If you don't need it now, you could find you need it much sooner than you think.

If you have already built the entity to attract your mate, you're half-way there—you can use the entity and all the other preliminary work, too. The preparation for this ritual begins by adopting the ad man's point of view in packaging your product just as we did for the lover-attracting ritual. But this time we need you to produce a second in-depth study—of all the strong and positive qualities of your mate. In this work, try to remember all the wonderful things about the person that attracted you in the first place, then add lots of new good qualities that your mate has developed along the way. Note the emphasis on the positive. Take care that you don't sit there criticizing your mate; this would have a very detrimental effect on your love renewal rite. So work to let your appreciation of the good qualities of your mate renew *your* enthusiasm for the relationship, and produce a good list to be programmed into your entity.

Take both lists to your altar area, along with the same set of materials we used for the lover-attracting rite. After your joy ritual, begin to work on your entity. If you are building a new one because you didn't need the lover-attracting ritual, go through the whole building process just as we gave it. But if you already have built the entity, go through the same procedure, but instead of words like "I endow the entity with," say "I feed the entity with," or "I nourish the entity with."

As you complete your entity, program it again with your well-thought-out set of good qualities, then describe the good qualities of your mate in equally enthusiastic terms. Finally give the entity specific instructions: "Your purpose from now until I may give you changes is to strive to amplify the good qualities of each of us while helping any negative qualities to slip away into nothingness. You will inspire each of us to be especially nice, appealing and erotic to the other, with a magnificent renewal of the spontaneity and love between us that feeds on each fresh bit of enthusiasm and happy experience to grow ever more wonderful as time passes. I will do my best to give you my full cooperation, and will sit here to meet with you each day so that you may give me guidance and instruction as may be necessary. You will get great pleasure out of your work with us and joyously share our love and fulfillment. Thank you, and so mote it be."

As always, sit quietly after giving the instructions to be receptive to any guidance or comments, either from your entity or your helpers in the spirit world. Then when you are ready, again thank all who helped and shared with you, snuff your candles, and return to your normal routine.

WONDERFUL RESULTS FROM THE GNOSTIC LOVE RENEWAL RITE

Charlotte and Jerry met, wooed and married in a space of about six weeks. It was the second marriage for each, but it very shortly developed a real rough spot. Let's let Charlotte's report explain: "We had been married only a couple of weeks when Jerry's impotence problem got squarely in the way. Yes, he told me about it before the wedding, but in our wild six weeks of courtship it certainly was not in evidence—quite the contrary! But after his first 'failure,' as he put it, he seemed to come apart as a lover. I tried to get him to seek medical and/or psychiatric help, but he would have no part of it. And my life became one giant frustration. After about six months of trying everything I could think of and getting almost no affection, and absolutely no sex, I turned as a last resort to the Gnostic Love Renewal Rite.

"Since I encountered this work after I was already married, I had not built the lover-attracting entity. So I started from scratch and built and programmed my entity to revitalize my love life. It was easy to feed the entity my husband's strong points, then I added a special programming instruction, 'Your purpose is to make Jerry affectionate and a confident lover again.' The whole ritual was very pleasant and I enjoyed visualizing our affection and lovemaking as it had been before the marriage. It was shortly after three in the afternoon when I completed the ritual. As I sat in silence, I got a strong urge to get a bit of the remaining sun. We have a terrace where we can sunbathe nude without being seen by the neighbors, so I went there and of course took off all my clothes. I guess I dropped off to sleep, and what a wonderful awakening! Jerry came home and looked around for me—and somehow everything hit him just right. We had the very best sexual encounter of our relationship up to that point! It was especially wonderful after those awful six months of being affection and sex starved. I talk to my love renewal entity every day, thanking and encouraging it. We're approaching our first anniversary, and everything is truly wonderful. My loving thanks to all."

During the research for this book I also had what I call the classic encounter. A very nice lady, whom we will just call Mary, came to see me. She said, "I want you to use your psychic powers and tell me if my husband has a mistress."

I smiled and responded, "Tell me, how's your sex life these days?"

And here came the classic response, "What do you expect after 28 years?"

So I gave her my equally classic response, "I don't need to be psychic. Your husband has a mistress." Then we talked about the Gnostic Love Renewal Rite and she agreed to try it. This is her report:

"You shocked me with your flip response to my very serious question, but I thought it over and realized you were right. I decided that considering our boredom with each other during the last too many years, if he didn't have a mistress he should have. So I went about the entity building with plenty of enthusiasm, and of course I let it give me several suggestions on spicing up my appearance, and especially some on how to send my husband off to the office and greet him when he got home. I also felt I was following directions when I went to a local bookstore to get some of the newer books on sexual expression. And frankly I learned a lot—it's amazing how completely my sex education was neglected in my almost 'holier than thou' upbringing.

"The results didn't come all at once, but I did seem to get a little extra attention and response for everything I tried to do to improve things between us. Now I've been working with my love renewal entity for about four months and the metamorphosis has been magnificent. My husband is breaking his habit of scheduling evening meetings for his staff, and he is planning a trip for us—almost a world tour that he has titled our second honeymoon. I am no longer suspicious and insecure. I have my husband and he likes it! Thanks to all of my energy transformer friends, my entity, and to you, Al, for the help."

Of course the love renewal rite is equally useful to men as this report from J.R. shows: "We have been married about 12 years. Not long ago I realized that we were quite completely taking each other for granted—or should I say that the marriage had degenerated to something between mediocre and humdrum. The Gnostic Love Renewal Rite seemed just right, so I gathered my goodies and headed to the altar to see what I might accomplish. I enjoyed the entity building and programming, then during the silent period I got some interesting inputs.

"There was a realization that I had been way less than attentive, and this must have contributed to Barbara's neglect of her appearance and the house. I promised to do my part and urged my entity to dig into its work. The result was most interesting; it sort of turned into a mutual 'be nice to each other' tribal rite. First we started paying more attention to each other, then doing nice little things. Then we had a revival of the sexual relationship that has carried us to magnificent new heights of mutual pleasure. I am happy to report that my marriage is no longer humdrum; rather it has become exciting and happy again. I will work with my entity indefinitely to assure the continued growth and happiness of my marriage."

CARE AND FEEDING OF YOUR LOVER-ATTRACTING/LOVE RENEWAL ENTITY

How long should your helpful entity last? And how long should you reasonably expect a better and better feeling about your marriage or lover? In both cases the answer is "until you become complacent." Your lover-attracting/love renewal entity was created out of the energies of happiness and love. It feeds on these energies and grows ever stronger as it vicariously shares your happiness and fulfillment; that is its purpose. Compliment it regularly and feed it with joy. And let your love life grow ever richer and more fulfilling.

GNOSTIC MAGIC MIND JOGGERS

1. Begin preparations to attract your wonderful lover by using the mirror exercise to pinpoint your strong points—what you have to *give*.
2. Study the idea of creating your own entity as part of the preparation for the Gnostic Lover-Attracting Ritual.
3. Enjoy creating and programming your entity as you follow the simple ritual. Then let the entity lead and help you to happiness.
4. With a well-built entity, nothing is impossible; cooperate with it and learn as you fill your life with happy companionship.
5. It may be even more important to renew a slipping love affair. For this, use the Gnostic Love Renewal Rite—it works wonders.
6. Care for your lover-attracting/love renewal entity, feed it with joy and happiness, and it will serve you extremely well indefinitely.

10

Gnostic Magic: Key to Extra Zest, Good Luck, and a Perfect Spirit Lover

In all of your studies of the occult, metaphysics, magic and the like, you will never find anything so completely wonderful as a good relationship with your perfect spirit lover. Imagine a being who has loved you deeply since before you were born, indeed who has loved you for countless centuries—sometimes sharing the life experience with you in physical bodies, and at other times loving you perhaps even more completely while one of you lived in a physical body and the other existed simply in the finer vibrations that we recognize as the world of spirit beings.

With never the slightest twinge of jealousy or possessiveness or the least interference with your physical love life, you will enjoy the experience of being completely loved. Yes, you will find many material benefits from this marvelous relationship, too, but even without that part, you would certainly agree that this relationship is a super highlight to this and all your previous lives! I have suggested at times that you might want to skip a chapter and come back to it at some later time. But this one is not to be skipped; it is the bridge to a whole series of magnificent and "unbelievably wonderful" experiences.

WHY A SPIRIT LOVER? IS IT SAFE?

You may wonder at the use of so many superlatives in the opening paragraph of this chapter. Let me try to explain it from the personal level. During my slightly over 50 years in this earthly sojourn I have led what some would call a bit of a wild life. I have had three lovely wives with many fascinating lovers sandwiched in between. I enjoy life quite fully, but in all honesty I would have to say that my meeting with my own spirit lover and the subsequent development of that relationship stands out as something super special. I could easily use just my personal experiences to give all the illustrations and examples needed in this chapter, but I won't. I want to keep sharing the experiences of people I've had the privilege of working with, so you can be sure that these manifestations are not the exception belonging to one strange character, but are indeed completely available to you.

Now why a spirit lover? Next to one's parents who provided your physical vehicle and helped you care for it until you were big enough to handle it yourself, the most important of life's relationships are with your lover(s). Most people are more or less starved for real affection for the greater part of their lives—and the tragic part about this is it is completely unnecessary! I have never been able to understand why the occult and spiritualist writers in the "golden period" between 1890 and 1930 completely avoided the subject of the spirit lover. But that was a time of a stilted Victorian approach to anything that even slightly suggested sex, so we must not fault our older teachers, just recognize that in the here and now it is not necessary to be limited by *their* hangups. Now let's directly answer the question of *why*: to me it is simply that the phenomenon already exists, the experience is ecstatically positive, it hurts no one, and it is very good for you—so why not?

In terms of safety, the probing student may bring up old terms like *incubus* and *succubus*, and such things certainly do exist even in today's society, but they are not at all related to the beautiful spirit lover experience. However, *astral* sex is completely possible and normal with your spirit lover, but that is getting ahead of ourselves.) Let's state specifically that if an entity attempts sex with you while you are fully in your physical body, reject it at once as probably an incubus/ succubus problem which has the disadvantage of happening at the entity's convenience and not being able to be turned off. With only that one small (and quite infrequent) caveat, I can assure you that even your early attempts to meet and enjoy your spirit lover are infinitely safer than going out for a Sunday drive.

WHAT YOUR SPIRIT LOVER CAN DO FOR YOU—AND WHO IS HE (OR SHE)?

The very great degree of a spirit entity's ability to influence the three-dimensional or material world is of course not at all recognized by science (as yet), but that does *not* make it any less real or less useful! Gifts of money and fine jewelry, introductions to the "right people," protection from and avoidance of accidents or other disasters—literally ANYTHING that a person in a physical body can do for you is completely within the realm of the natural ability of your spirit lover. But I want to emphasize here, as I did in our last chapter, that the material benefits you will most certainly receive are NOT the proper reason to seek this most beautiful of relationships. We seek this form of companionship for the sheer joy of the relationship itself, then accept the material gifts graciously because we know that it gives our lover pleasure to give them—and in turn we lovingly give of ourselves, enjoying the ever more beautiful rapport and the intimacies of honest affection. And none of this in any way detracts from your "normal" existence because it takes place mostly while your physical body is getting its needed rest in the state called sleep.

As to who is your spirit lover, we want to avoid the ever-present tendency toward an ego trap. When people start looking at their past lives, they all want to be Napoleon, DaVinci, St. Paul or the like, never a galley slave, and the wish fulfillment part of your mind can be strong enough to blot out the truth in such circumstances, with the same problem slopping over if you try to get all the name, date, and place information about your spirit lover. Besides, that part of the "who" is totally insignificant. Your spirit lover is undoubtedly a person who loved you in a past life (or many past lives) when both of you had physical bodies. Right now you have a body and your spirit lover does not, but the infinity of time promises that the roles will be reversed sooner or later (or even have been before this life of yours). When the working rapport with your spirit lover is well established, there will be plenty of time to reminisce about past lives together and learn a lot about yourself in that happy sharing of experience. But even then if your spirit lover tells you that you were Cleopatra, Caesar, Joan of Arc, a Greek god or the like, take it as a lover's compliment, *not* historical fact. But enough of the introductory ideas; it's time to go about contacting your very own spirit lover—after one tiny further comment: that is there should be absolutely no interference or disturbance of your marital or other material plane love affairs, except perhaps to make them better, too. From a spirit lover, there is no jealousy, only the desire to help you make your life richer and fuller on ALL planes of existence.

HOW TO ATTRACT YOUR PERFECT
SPIRIT LOVER

I used the word "attract" here because our materially oriented minds would naturally think that way. Actually a better term would be to recognize or re-establish good communications with your spirit lover. To begin, picture the most beautiful and attractive person you can imagine; try not to make it a celebrity, movie star, or anybody you have known; rather do it in the abstract. When we were adolescents the term "dream girl" or "dream man" pretty well described the picture we're looking for here. In fact, during that period of your life, the mental picture of your dream mate quite probably was a form of contact with your spirit lover, but like all other forms of psychic contact, you were educated to believe that it was "all your imagination," so the process of "growing up" literally took it away from you. Thus we see another instance of the significance of Jesus' comment, "Except ye become as a little child. ... " And we can easily understand that the first step in recontacting your spirit lover is to let your imagination or "daydreaming nature" bring back the feeling that there really is someone out there (only this time a spirit being) who is totally the lover of your dreams.

We will use the Gnostic Spirit Lover Ritual to perfect and enhance your contact, but it is a good idea to spend a week in preparation by using this simple exercise. Each night, when you lie down to go to sleep (and if you take an extra nap somewhere along the line, then too) try to remember the dream lover as you pictured him (or her) back when you were about 12 years old. Be 12 with all the innocence and beautiful dreams of a super happy life that so naturally go with it, and expect to meet your lover in your dreams. Drift off to sleep in that state of happy anticipation, and at least twice during the week, you should have a very lovely "dream" where you renew your ancient love affair.

If you don't remember a dream or two during the week, don't be disappointed, I guarantee you that something happened; it's just the matter of bringing it back into waking consciousness that is the problem. Either way, try to write a love poem or love song to your spirit lover at a point where it feels good to you. I sing love songs to my spirit lover in the shower many mornings, especially after a particularly wonderful visit the previous night, and SO WILL YOU! What we are trying to suggest here is that you let yourself go and deliberately become a "romantic." Let the ideas of innocent and pure love fill your life expression with the special zest that somehow gets you walking about six inches off the ground. When you have built that mood, you're ready to bring the relationship to greater reality by using the Gnostic Spirit Lover Ritual.

I stopped to rest here as I was writing this, and my own spirit lover, Karakassa, asked me to share with you my love song to her as part of the explanation and setting of the mood for the Spirit Lover Ritual. I borrowed the tune to the beautiful song, "Mona Lisa":

> Karakassa, Karakassa, I adore you.
> How I long to kiss your lips and see you smile.
> Karakassa, Karakassa, I implore you,
> Won't you help me come to see you for a while.
> Karakassa, Karakassa, Spirit Lover,
> I know you're with me and we're never far apart.
> You are warm, you are real, Karakassa,
> How I long to hold you closer to my heart.

By a strange "coincidence," you can borrow this one if you haven't written one of your own. The words "spirit lover" have the same number of syllables and meter as "Karakassa," so by making the substitution, you can have a reasonable love song of your own—but this is offered only as a secondary alternative to your own creation.

All of this is in preparation for your Gnostic Spirit Lover Ritual. You will understand that this is a joyous occasion with a built-in party atmosphere. So we should prepare for a party with wine (or grapejuice) and almonds (or other goodies), just as we do for the ritual of joy. Candles and incense, love oil, the ritual of joy preparations, and your love poem or love song go along to your altar for the Gnostic Spirit Lover Ritual, but in this case you will clearly understand that the most important ingredients are YOU and your spirit lover.

PERFORMING THE GNOSTIC SPIRIT LOVER RITUAL

Be sure you are in a happy mood, but still sprinkle salt water all around your altar area before you start. Light your candles and incense, and anoint your brow, throat and heart centers with your oil—and put a little behind each ear, too, just for the romance of it. Now begin a brief ritual of joy to reestablish a solid contact with your energy transformer personality friends. When this part is finished, announce aloud, "Now good friends, it's time to focus our attention on this party's guest of honor, my spirit lover. I ask all of you to help me rebuild the rapport and beautiful communications— ever better than it has been with my spirit lover before."

Now use your healthy imagination (if necessary) to picture the bright aura of your spirit lover standing behind you, touching your shoulders with his (or her) hands. Then lift your cup to toast your spirit lover and speak aloud: "To my spirit lover, a special welcome as honored guest at our party." Then sing or read your love poem to your spirit lover, several times. This is one of those times when I hope you are working at your altar as I do, in the clothing you were wearing when your physical body first entered the world from your mother's womb. You may feel some nice responses anyway, but if there is no clothing in the way, at some point you will feel a loving electric-like touch across your shoulders that generally sends a happy shiver all the way down your spine. Or sometimes there is a delicious feeling of being hugged all over. This shivery, electric-like response is a very important part of my morning and evening ritual work, and I trust it will become similarly important to you. But patience and the idea of wooing are the order of the day. If you don't notice a response at first, just assume that it was so subtle you missed it. Time and practice (and wooing) will bring that part into ever more wonderful reality. Whether or not you felt a response, when you have finished singing your love poem, speak aloud to your spirit lover: "I fervently desire to improve our communication and rapport. Please help me to visit you on your own plane of life while my physical body is in its state of sleep tonight. Help me to be ever more wide awake, to participate, and to remember ever more of our happy experiences together."

Then toast your spirit lover again and sit quietly to see if there is any more guidance, or some love vibrations to soak up. When you feel that it is finished, thank everyone who participated, snuff your candles and go back to your normal routine.

One added comment: I prefer to do this ritual just at bedtime so its happiness and the contact itself will pass freshly with me into the sleep state to enhance the waking up on the astral levels to enjoy my spirit lover more fully. But do it whenever it feels right to you—and as often as you wish.

WHAT TO EXPECT FROM YOUR GNOSTIC SPIRIT LOVER RITUAL

Jerry N. had this to report: "Al, I had forgotten about my adolescent dream girl until you reminded me. As you know I'm in my fifties and quite happily married, so I knew there was nothing of a wish fulfillment or neurotic danger here. But as I thought about it, I got a kind of a thrill at the memory, so I decided to try the ritual. I have always called my dream girl Laura, and it worked in all right, so I borrowed your love song/ poem and took my wine and other goodies to my altar on a night when my wife was tired and had gone to bed early. The ritual was enjoyable, as they always are, and when I tried to picture my spirit lover's aura close behind me there was some kind of a tingly response, even before I started to sing her my love song. As I continued, it felt like someone was pouring buckets of soft electricity on my head, shoulders and down my spine—honestly, I tingled and had goose bumps all over, and, *that* is definitely NOT my imagination! That night I had a magnificent time in my 'dreams' sharing love and affection with Laura. Near the end she told me I had been too wrapped up in my business and not attentive enough to my wife. She said she would give me a gentle shove by providing a bit of a windfall out of which I was to buy my wife a nice present. Believe it or not, the next afternoon I got a phone call that resulted in a $25,000 commission for about five minutes' work. As the deal was concluded, I got those buckets of soft electricity all over me again so I knew this was from Laura. I did my part and bought my wife a nice diamond necklace as an 'unbirthday' present. What can I say, Al—with some regular prodding from Laura, my married life is happier than I had ever dreamed possible, and my sleep time is nothing short of delicious. You said that getting a rapport with one's spirit lover is the most beautiful of all occult experiences, but I say it's better than that! Words will never do the experience justice."

Catherine S. had this experience: "I am young (my middle 20's) and was living alone, so the idea of the Gnostic Spirit Lover Ritual had plenty of appeal to me. I had enjoyed my earlier Gnostic ritual work, so approached this one in a spirit of good fellowship. I won't say I actually saw an aura behind me, but I sure *felt* a presence and a *touch*! It was a thoroughly exhilarating experience, followed by an even more wonderful 'dream' experience. Out there in my spirit lover's arms, he told me I was too lonely and should have a companion in a physical body. He said give me a week and I'll arrange an introduction. And some introduction! He was calling on my boss and somehow tripped and fell literally *right at my feet*. As I leaned over to help him up, I felt the touch of my spirit lover, and HE did, too! The courtship was short, but lovely. We were married just three weeks from the day he fell at my feet. Before the wedding I told him about my spirit lover and our introduction. He calls me his love witch! But always with a smile and so tenderly. We are leading something like a charmed life. Whenever something starts to go wrong, my spirit lover gives me instructions or simply volunteers to 'head the trouble off at the pass,' and things are constantly super for both of us—or should I say all three of us. My husband is about ready to try to meet his spirit lover, too, and I'm sure that will add even more enjoyment to the whole set of relationships."

DEVELOPING THE HAPPY RELATIONSHIP WITH YOUR SPIRIT LOVER

The keynote to developing and maintaining an ever more wonderful relationship with your spirit lover is best understood by paraphrasing the oft-quoted words from President Kennedy's inaugural address: We would say, ask not what your spirit lover can do for you, but what you can do for your spirit lover. Understand that here is a being quite totally interested and dedicated to helping you make the most of your life, both spiritually and materially. Your spirit lover will naturally want to do nice things for you and give you nice gifts—but not so much that it saps your incentive or "spoils you."

In turn you should regularly ask what you can do to return the spirit of the gifts and help. And there may be those times when the answer comes as an urge to do something special to help a fellow being along the way, but the constant element will be the urging to live up to your own full potential. This is not to imply that you should live a Spartan, out-of-balance existence in any shape or form. Rather it implies enjoying life to the fullest as part of the balanced approach to fulfilling your various potentials. You may be urged to rest or play when you have been overdoing on the work side, just as you will be nudged along to industriousness if you have exhibited a lack in that area. Your willingness to "listen" and take good advice will help keep up the relationship almost as much as your romanticism; again it is a matter of enjoying life to the fullest by accomplishing where you should and playing where that is in order, and by mixing the two virtually to the consternation of the stuffier people around you.

Share as much as possible of all of this with your physical plane mate, but begin very cautiously so as not to expose your spirit lover to ridicule or jealousy. You know that there is room in your heart for both a spirit lover and an earthly mate—but is your mate ready to accept the idea? If not, make the introduction a gradual process, by "jokingly" giving credit to your spirit lover for the nice things that happen to you and your spouse. Adopt the basic idea that silence is better than open misunderstanding, and learn to follow the advice of your spirit lover in the care and feeding of your earthly mate. Thus in time you will be able to fully enjoy and share all of life's richest experiences with both your spirit and your physical mate. Then in time you will have the delight of introducing your physical mate to his (or her) spirit lover, so the four of you can enjoy the fullness of life together.

We have barely scratched the surface of the potential of the relationship with your spirit lover. This one is your natural gateway to the pleasant give and take with the wonderful world of spirit. We will strive to show you much more of this aspect in our next chapter, but meanwhile let's close this one by sharing one more report of the joys of the spirit lover contact. This one is from Janet U.: "It was right after my husband served me with divorce papers that I decided to use the Gnostic Spirit Lover Ritual. Honestly I was seeking consolation and comfort, and I hoped that somehow I could avoid the divorce that way. Because I was upset (I see this now in retrospect), it was not all that easy to make the contact with my spirit lover, but I kept trying for I guess ten or more straight nights. Finally I 'imagined' I felt a faint but oh so loving touch on my shoulder during the ritual and I accepted the meeting very gratefully.

"That night I also met my spirit lover (I call him Claude) in my dream state. And it was quite a surprise! Claude told me I had outgrown my husband, so I should accept a reasonable settlement and let him go. I accepted the advice and so instructed my attorney the next morning. Just a week later I was in my attorney's office to sign the necessary papers, but there was a delay because he was tied up in court longer than he had expected. A stranger passed the time of day with me; he was also waiting to sign some papers. And as we talked, I kept getting the feeling of loving caresses from Claude. So when he asked me to join him for dinner, I did so without hesitation. Claude is a wonderful matchmaker! My new husband is everything I could ask for in a man; he even listened eagerly when I gave him the first indication about my spirit lover, Claude. He asked if I could help him to meet his spirit lover also, and this time the ritual worked the first time. I guess there was enough love and fun there to make it easy. Anyway, we each know that we were led to each other to be real helpmates and to share our spiritual seeking as well as our material world progress together. We join in the Spirit Lover Ritual at least twice a week, often as a prelude to some magnificent lovemaking that somehow seems to also involve both of our spirit lovers in a super special experience. We are happy and prosperous, and never a day goes by without one or the other of us getting some kind of a special gift or bit of exceptionally useful guidance from our spirit lover. You know about all the wonderful doors it is opening for us. Thank you, Al, for the teaching and you, Claude, for the joy of your love."

GNOSTIC MAGIC MIND JOGGERS

1. The most wonderful of all your occult, metaphysical or magical experiences will be your meeting with and subsequent relationship with your spirit lover.
2. Your spirit lover exists whether you pay attention or not, and the development of the relationship is quite safe. It's natural and wonderful to do it.
3. Your spirit lover can bring you material gifts and financial help, and no doubt will, but this is not the primary reason for seeking the relationship. Rather it should be for the sheer joy of sharing the love experience with this most special of beings.
4. Try to avoid stereotypes like movie stars, folk heroes or old acquaintances as you romanticize and remember the man or woman of your adolescent dreams. This was often a form of real contact with your spirit lover.
5. Use the romantic dream idea for a week or so in preparation for the Gnostic Spirit Lover Ritual. And let your romantic nature write love songs or love poems to this wonderful spirit being.
6. Approach the Gnostic Spirit Lover Ritual as a party with your spirit lover as the guest of honor. Enjoy the meeting and let it enhance your dream experiences also.
7. Nurture and participate in the development of the happy relationship with your spirit lover. There will be many immediate benefits, and we will find this relationship a very useful bridge to the work of our next chapter.

11

Attract and Summon Gnostic Magic Help from the Spirit World

Once you have met your spirit lover, there is no more doubt about the existence of the spirit world. Then the immediate question becomes, "Is there a way that I can relate to the world of spirit to provide practical mutual benefits?" Certainly the loving caresses and happy relationship with your spirit lover have removed any traces of fear of such contacts—and I trust have already given you a few nice tastes of the potential benefits.

Just as in the material world, there are choices—potential associates to be cultivated and enjoyed, and some that are best avoided. In the world that you're "used to," we make our choices of associates for a variety of reasons—business, social, spiritual, or a wonderful form of "chemistry" called "we just like each other." Similarly you will find that your spirit lover wants to share his (or her) friends with you, so the initial expansion of your spirit contacts will be on the friendship level. And through these friends and your lover you will find yourself meeting advisers, helpers and experts in fields of endeavor that are similar to or complementary to your own. Let's consider that part first.

EXPERTS IN FINANCE, MEDICINE, SCIENCE AND THE LIKE ARE AVAILABLE TO HELP YOU FROM SPIRIT

Would you like to have the best financiers of history for your personal advisors? Or advice and tangible medical help from the greatest doctors of the past who have indeed kept up with and nurtured the latest developments of today? Or the best in scientific and engineering help and advice? Certainly the price is right—NO CHARGE. The help you get comes to you primarily because the spirit people who participate are doing it for the sheer joy of helping, but partly because you have made yourself cooperative and deserving of their attention and help. There is no skill or discipline left out; literally *anything* or any subject in which you need help has active, up-to-date practitioners in the spirit world. You have only to learn the proper ways to ask for help and to thank your spirit friends for the magnificent good that comes to you. Naturally there are Gnostic Magic Rituals for this, but we need a bit of preliminary work on when and in what situation your plea for help will receive the most full and favorable attention.

In the course of your earth life this far, you have received far more requests for help that you have responded favorably to, indeed far more than you had time or resources to handle. Now think of the literally millions of pleas for help that pass into the spirit world in the form of fervent prayer and cries of anguish as well as carefully structured magical invocations. How are the priorities set, and by whom? The basic answer resides in an intelligent analysis of your own experience. If you pass an obvious wino on the street and he *politely* asks you for a handout, you may give him a small gift (knowing that you're not really helping him, but letting the compassion of the moment prevail); but if someone you know and respect has a real opportunity or need and asks for your help, you will figure ways to provide *substantial* help within the scope of your abilities.

The same is true of the spirit beings—your personality and outlook don't change that much upon the surrender of your physical body! So you must take care that you don't look like a lush looking for a handout, but like a substantial being striving to get ahead—so that by helping YOU, the spirit is honestly helping to uplift a good portion of mankind. But here we must not insult the spirit's intelligence—as in the classic case in my own experience where a woman wrote and asked me to use my psychic powers to send her a million dollars so she could use fifty thousand of it to help the "poor Navajos."

Your drive and sincere desire to uplift yourself and get ahead provide the currency or attractiveness that singles YOU out for high priority help. And in another very real sense there is a patina of omnipresence and omnipotence to spirit which guarantees that you will be heard and helped because you are sincere in trying to grow and learn along with your striving. As you become an accomplished Gnostic Magician, able to help yourself more and more, you will grow into the "big time" where the spirit help is less frequent but much more significant. Thus you approach the goal of being a true Master of your fate, in cooperation with your wonderful friends and helpers in the spirit world.

THE GNOSTIC INFORMAL APPROACH TO
SPIRIT CONTACT AND HELP

By this point, you know that my approach to all of life is as informal as possible. So it's natural that I would suggest a totally informal approach to your spirit contact. You have met your spirit lover and hopefully shared many happy experiences by now. And this is clearly on an informal level. In our opening section, I suggested that your spirit lover would want to share her (or his) friends with you; that is the basis of the informal approach. Begin by attuning with your spirit lover and simply speaking aloud: "My lover, I am ready to meet some of your friends. Shall we extend our party to include them now, or shall I wait until tomorrow to give you a chance to invite people?"

If you are accustomed to seeing aura, you will usually see an extra one or two coming close to you at that point. There

may be a feeling of an introduction, like "Al, this is John," or
"Barbara, I'd like you to meet my lover, Al." At first this will
usually take place at your altar, and I would expect you to
have something of a joy ritual going, so you can respond by
toasting the new spirit acquaintance and saying aloud, "It's a
pleasure to meet a friend of my lover. Hi!"

Your spirit lover is intimately acquainted with your
spiritual and economic needs, so he (or she) is apt to very
quickly bring in an expert in the field of your needed help. But
it's good not to try to force this part. Just relax and honestly
try to enjoy and get to know each spirit that is brought to you.
If you feel that nothing happened on your first request, don't
be disappointed; just tell your spirit lover that you'll try again
tomorrow after there has been time to contact and invite
friends.

During or just after one of these friendly sessions, you
will begin to get fresh ideas or bits of inspiration in one or
more areas of your personal need. Here a bit of common sense
is in order. We are taught in the Bible, "Test the spirits that
they are of God." Taken literally, this can be confusing or even
insulting to your new spirit acquaintance. But it is altogether
proper to go through a period of getting to know a spirit friend
just as you would get to know a new friend in a physical body.
Learn his (or her) hang-ups and areas of weakness, as well as
the areas of expertise, so you will know which advice is
professional and which is the guesswork of an amateur. This
judgment factor will be your most important tool for effective
use of the help available to you from spirit.

Here many of you will be asking, "But how do I go about
conversing with a spirit?" You are off to a good start by simply
feeling the presence and loving caress of your spirit lover. Just
as with people in bodies of skin and bone, the close proximity
of one person feels somewhat different from another, and a
little practice will let that feeling quite completely identify
the visiting spirit as the same fellow who joined you at the
altar last night or three weeks ago. Next comes the matter of
actual interchange of ideas, and again we will learn to rely on
our *feeling* nature for the critical tools or aids to confidence

and accuracy. By far the most common form of receiving communication from spirit entities is by simple thought transference (telepathy if you both had physical bodies). When you speak aloud, your thought is projected strongly and clearly enough for the spirit beings around you to "hear" and understand, and their standard reaction is to pop an answering thought into your head. Even if you have never spoken aloud to (or *at*, if you like) a spirit, I assure you that you *have* received many communications in that simple form of an idea "popped" into your head. Now it becomes a matter of "feeling" the difference between *your* thinking process and an idea or thought directed to you from an outside source.

Just recognizing that these things take place is the beginning. Then many times during the day when you "get an idle thought," feel it mentally to see if it was "yours" or was sent to you. As you experiment this way for a few weeks, you will develop an excellent degree of accuracy and find that you are able to carry on quite an effective conversation with one or more spirit beings as long as the subject matter is not highly emotional to you. Practice this simple process until you know you're good at it; there will be many benefits in the form of inspiration and useful information for you from the practice; and you will need the ability all the more for those times when you feel it necessary to organize a more formal conference session with your most important spirit guides and experts.

WHAT TO EXPECT FROM THE INFORMAL APPROACH

This report from J.W. shows how a few friendly chats can serve to keep you out of trouble: "I had been to my altar for a brief Gnostic ritual, and as has become my habit I continued some friendly chatter with my spirit friends as I aimlessly wandered into the den. I got an urge to look over my modest stock portfolio, so I got it out, all the while making what you could only call small talk with the spirit beings. As I looked over the short list, I heard a spirit voice for the first time. It was as if someone standing right next to me spoke quite loudly, 'Sell that one tomorrow!' I wondered if it was uneasiness because that stock at its then market value represented slightly over half of my portfolio value. Anyhow, next day I put in a sell order at market to be sure of execution. And in just about two weeks after I got my settlement check from my broker, the big scandal broke. All trading was suspended in the stock. It turned out to be one of the biggest fraud scandals in history, and I'm not sure but that those caught holding the stock found it totally worthless. The net result to me was slightly over $32,000 in my bank account instead of a few stock certificates to use for bathroom wallpaper. You KNOW how enthusiastically I thanked my spirit people for days after the story came out!"

There is a lot of good humor and fun in the friendly give and take with your spirit friends, too, as this bit of feedback from B.G. will help you to see: "I really enjoy the relaxed, almost idle chatting with my spirit friends. And they are always helping me to find misplaced keys, papers and the like. But I had one recently that made me laugh so hard I just have to share it with you. I had been presented with an investment 'opportunity' that seemed to have a fantastic promise of really exciting returns. It sounded very good and I was just about to jump into it. Then I was enthusiastically telling the one I have come to know as my spirit financial advisor about it when—understand that I almost never get a real picture inside my head—suddenly I did see a bright and clear picture of a turtle standing on its hind legs with its back toward me. He twisted his head around and winked at me and in thought he very clearly said, 'Ha! Just remember that I licked that flighty son-of-a-gun rabbit!' I got the message and did not make the investment. I had forgotten about it until I got today's paper and read the story of the busting of a racket—it was the exact 'investment opportunity' the turtle picture had warned me against. I had another good laugh as I thanked my spirit friend for saving me my $10,000!"

Myrna R. was in a bit of a quandary that was happily resolved by a friendly chat with her spirit friends. Let's let her tell her story: "I was lonely and having a hard time making ends meet, when suddenly I encountered a new dilemma. I had been casually dating two different guys, but both relationships heated up at the same time. Each man asked me to move in with him for a short trial of the relationship before marriage—and they asked me within 24 hours of each other. I was confused by the two relationships and instinctively asked each one to continue as we were for a week or two while I thought it over. I was dating each man three nights a week, so on my 'night off' I was mulling it all over and talking more to myself than to my spirit friends. All at once there was a loud knock on my coffee table, almost as if someone had hit it with a hammer, and at the same instant came an unreasonably strong fear of J. I thought about it for a few minutes, then thanked my spirit people for the warning. In truth I felt slightly more in love with B. anyway, but J's glamour had kept me from being sure. The following weekend I did move in with B. and it quickly became a really dream relationship. We were married after just three weeks of the trial—we both knew! Now after a month of being a happily married person I got a sudden stimulus to write you about it. In today's paper I saw a picture of J.—he had been arrested as a dealer in illicit drugs. I have a double thank-you for my spirit people. One for steering me to my lovely husband, and another for keeping me away from the disaster that I might have had with J."

THE GNOSTIC SPIRIT CONFERENCE INVITATION RITE

In all areas of life we find some people who like to get their work with others accomplished almost totally on the informal basis, while others prefer to work in the atmosphere of a meeting, conference, or seminar. Obviously both approaches have their place in an active life expression, so it is time now to explore the ideas of calling and/or attending meetings of spirit people that will be helpful to you in your problem solving or knowledge seeking endeavors. You will recognize that there are two specific steps to the more formal work. First, the meeting must be called for a specific time and place, with appropriate notification or invitation to the interested parties; then second, the parties actually gather and share their information or conduct their business at the appointed time and place.

Just as part of life, you should converse regularly with your spirit friends on the informal level—and you will find that this is enough to get you sound advice and help with most of your problems. But at those times when you don't seem to get enough of an answer or your regular band of spirit friends doesn't seem to have the answer, it is quite reasonable and practical to ask for a special meeting where the necessary experts can be invited. If you have several unrelated but chronic problems, it is also reasonable to try to handle all or at least most of them at one meeting. Thus your initial preparation before planning to issue the invitations should be to plan an agenda. Write down the list of major problems in the order of their importance to you at the time, and work the list into a handwritten invitation that should read something like this:

"Greetings to my spirit lover, teachers, guides and friends. I need your guidance and help and invite you to join me in a special conference on the following matters. [*Here copy your prepared agenda.*] Please invite and bring with you any beings who you feel have special expertise in one or more of these areas to help us. I will come to my altar for this purpose tomorrow at [*insert the exact time at which you will do the actual conference ritual*]. I look forward to our happy meeting and thank you all in advance for your wonderful help."

The Spirit Conference Invitation Rite itself should begin with the Gnostic Ritual of Joy to set the right mood for the invitation. Make your preparations, then go to your altar. After a happy ritual of joy, read your invitation aloud three times, then touch the corner of the paper to your candle and read it again just ahead of the flame—dropping it safely into your regular receptacle at the end. Then sit quietly for a few moments in case there might be an immediate message from your spirit friends. When you are ready, snuff your candles, thank everyone and go back to your normal routine. Then of course be sure to keep your appointment with your spirit friends the next day.

THE GNOSTIC SPIRIT CONFERENCE RITUAL

Take care to be on time and in a happy mood for your spirit conference ritual. In addition to routine preparation for the ritual of joy, be sure to take along pencil and paper so you can make notes, particularly if the ideas start coming wonderfully fast. Begin with a happy ritual of joy, being alert during this part, too, for bits of advice or powerful solutions that may be given to you. Let me digress for a moment to re-emphasize the significance of the light and happy approach. I just came away from a classic demonstration of this beautiful Gnostic principle that came about in a totally unplanned way. The experiment involved highly sophisticated brain wave measuring gear, chart recorder, oscilloscope, optical couplings and nicely scientific conditions. The brain patterns were not receptive to psychic inputs at first, and normal meditation and calming techniques seemed to help very little. But as soon as we started to gently tease the subject and clown around in the lab, the patterns of receptivity immediately showed up. The experiment was saved from failure by a touch of good humor!

This digression is important to the understanding of the rest of the ritual. You have greeted your spirit friends and advisers in the party atmosphere; keep that feeling of fun as you turn to the first subject on your agenda. Address the question to your friends, and KNOW that the answer is right there for you. The trick is to get your anxious "front mind" (or intellect) to relax enough to let the message through. In modern terms, this is a project of the right hemisphere (of the brain) requiring the pleasant diversion of the left hemisphere's attention so that the creative contact can be made and recognized. If you don't feel that you have received an answer, by all means don't get frustrated or up-tight about it. Instead, tease the situation gently, and joke a bit about learning not to appear such a clod about getting your messages. Play with each item on your agenda, and enjoy teasing about things. Very often you will get your answer out of your own mouth, recognizing something you thought you said in jest as the actual answer from your spirit friends. When you feel you have gone as far as you productively can, thank your spirit friends and invite them to give you any more data they have for you in the dream state that evening or as a "flash" of an idea whenever they can sneak it in to you. And stay constantly alert to *notice* the inputs. Meanwhile conclude the ritual with a few moments of silence and a big thank-you to your spirit friends, then snuff out your candles.

GETTING THE MOST OUT OF YOUR GNOSTIC SPIRIT CONFERENCE RITUALS

Your own special brand of humor will enhance this part of your work more than all the diligent application and earnest suplication in the world. Let's share J.D.'s report to help you understand: "You know the situation in aerospace. My career had taken a major setback and I found myself working as a 'slave' in a totally unrelated industry. Not only was the pay only about half of what I was used to, but the hours were terrible—so much so that I had not been able to figure any way to positively look for a better situation. In fact, I was so tired those days it was all I could do to muster enough strength for the spirit conference invitation rite and spirit conference ritual on successive nights. (I say nights, not evenings, because I generally got home from work around midnight and was expected back on the job before 8:00 A.M., so you see, 'slave' is a pretty appropriate term.)

"But I hadn't let the four months of 'slavery' get me down, so I teased my way through the invitation rite and really looked forward to the next evening. During the spirit conference itself, I got this wild urge. I sort of beckoned the whole group in very tight as as if I were going to whisper an exciting secret. And as the auras bent close to my own, I let out a combination of a bellow and a scream, 'HEEELLLPPP!'

Then I cracked up laughing, and felt that I really heard chuckles from the spirits close by. I felt a pat on my head as if to say, relax, we have it all under control. And sure enough, within three days I got a phone call from a former boss who had relocated and was building a new team. In just that one phone call we settled all the particulars—I was hired at 10% more than I had been making on the good job I had lost! And the hours are those of a human being, not a slave. It was a happy miracle, and I could tell by the pat on my head that my ridiculous sense of humor helped to speed up my spirit people and get me the help I so urgently needed. You *know* I still thank them all regularly for that one."

And when I asked half a dozen people what was their purpose the last time they asked for a spirit conference, all six immediately answered, "To find an important document, keys, etc.," so it is 100% typical to include this report from Sarah S.: "My husband teases me about my absent minded-ness, I guess only because he has so many examples to point at. This time it was getting serious, so I did the spirit conference rite asking for help to find a very important document, a valuable ring and my safe deposit box key. At the spirit conference ritual, it was natural to be jovial and tease myself. As I finished the joy ritual part, I sort of announced to the group of spirits, 'OK, here's your prize dingbat asking for a bit of help before my husband skins me alive.' So I asked where I could find the document, and immediately there was a flash of a box of odds and ends and papers I had under my sewing table—and I knew they were right. Then I said, 'Magnificent! Let's keep winning. Where's my diamond ring before Elmer finds out it's missing and hits the warpath?' This time I saw a picture inside my head. It was very bright and seemed to be inside a drawer. It was easy to recognize because that's the only red velvet lined drawer in the house. There was a bright, shiny object underneath the lining in the back; the lump was so tiny that by just looking without knowing you'd never spot it.

"Then there was a safe deposit box key that it would be most embarrassing to admit I'd lost, but by now it seemed easy. So I said, 'Let's keep up our win streak, how about the key?' This time there came only a pat on the head with a feeling of 'be patient,' so I said, 'OK, I guess you want to give me that one later—I'll be watching for your answer.' I thanked everybody and took off to retrieve the ring and document, and they were exactly where I expected them to be. And sure enough, that night I had a 'dream' where I was being teased about losing things, including my safe deposit box key. And of course it led me to the key the next morning. I often call my spirit band my set of 'dingbat bailer-outers.'"

I have lots of cases of spirit experts bringing very specific help, but they all seem too technical to fit in here. If you need very specialized help, the Gnostic Spirit Conference Ritual is certainly the place to start. I'll look forward to getting a very special "feedback" letter from YOU on your happy results!

GNOSTIC MAGIC MIND JOGGERS

1. The meeting with your spirit lover clearly eliminates all doubt about contact with the spirit world.
2. Your spirit lover will enjoy sharing his(or her) friends with you, and there is no nicer way to get used to spirit contact.
3. In times of interest or need, real experts in finance, medicine, or your special branch of science are not just available, but are happy to help as you approach them in the Gnostic traditions.
4. Your honest desire to get ahead and grow is the currency that "buys" your interested spirit help.
5. The informal approach will keep you a nice flow of solutions to most of your problems. Do get in the happy habit of chatting with your spirit friends in a friendly manner at all hours of the day and night.
6. If you don't get as much help as you need informally, set up the Gnostic Spirit Conference Invitation Rite, and the Spirit Conference Ritual. Performed in a party mood and a light, teasing manner, this will bring you ALL the help you could ever need.

12

Gnostic Magic Winning Secrets for Banishing Difficult Health Problems

Scattered around our globe in such diverse places as the Scandinavian countries, the Caribbean Islands, India, Hawaii and Southeast Asia, we find religious cults practicing the ancient art of firewalking—walking in bare feet for significant distances over hot lava or burning coals, with no pain and absolutely no damage to feet or legs. Of course there is some form of religious ecstasy or especially altered state of consciousness involved; a person does not perform such a feat or demonstration on a dare, and extremely rarely on a "two or three shows a day" basis.

Other special feats involving snakes or the drinking of deadly poisons show that there are no ill effects when done in what must be that same firewalking "mode" of beingness. I mention this as we open our special healing chapter to get your mind ready to accept the possibility that absolutely NOTHING is impossible! As we learn to fully attune ourselves with the primordial forces of the universe, it is completely possible to heal or restore anything that you or a loved one needs. But unless you TRY, you doom yourself or your loved one to accept the sentence of "death or permanent disability" that is all too often meted out by the well-meaning mundane or "non-magical" world.

THE GNOSTIC MAGICIAN RECOGNIZES NO IMPOSSIBLE SITUATION OR INCURABLE CONDITION

Let me continue this theme with a most enlightening personal experience. I was working with a very intense lady who was determined to "have" a specific gentleman "for her own" at all costs. She also happened to have a severe vision problem which was corrected with very powerful glasses. She often teased me by saying that when her glasses were off I became a sort of a bright blur to her, and of course the bifocal part was absolutely essential to her reading. But one afternoon she was in my office and had taken off her glasses to rest her eyes. We got into an excited discussion about some ritual work she wanted me to give her "to bring the man of my dreams running into my arms." I knew I had her *complete* attention, so I handed her a typewritten copy of the ritual and said, "Here it is, read it."

She took the piece of paper and started reading it aloud. She had read about two and a half long paragraphs *perfectly*, when she suddenly stopped and looked at me with a puzzled expression on her face. Then she exclaimed, "Oh my God, I'm not wearing my glasses!" And right then she could barely see the piece of paper as a fuzzy outline, much less make out one letter that was typed on it. I'd like to be able to tell you that from that session on she threw away her glasses and had perfect 20/20 vision, but it didn't happen. However those two and a half paragraphs read perfectly made a lasting impression on ME. It told me WITHOUT A SHADOW OF DOUBT that there is a part of YOU (and me, and everybody) that is capable of ANY achievement, healing or otherwise—that such a healing can be fleeting, temporary or *permanent*, depending only on the understanding and acceptance of the *person experiencing the healing*. So as I got deeper into my study of Gnostic Magic, it was easy to accept this part: TO AN

ACCOMPLISHED GNOSTIC MAGICIAN, THERE IS NO IMPOSSIBLE SITUATION OR INCURABLE CONDITION. And I hope I have been able to get this feeling strongly over to you, because it is the key to any and all "miracles" you will ever perform, now or in the distant future.

I get reports of varying degrees of healing "miracles" just about every day of the week; they range from the mundane to the super dramatic, but they are of small consolation to you if you still hurt, *except* as they can remind you that no cause is lost and spur you on to keep trying until you *win*! For most people, our work of Chapter 6, particularly the sacrifice ritual, proves enough to heal their existing maladies and propel them along a path of perfect health. If you have forgotten about or not yet used the Chapter 6 work, do review and USE it because it will set a solid Gnostic Magical Foundation for the more powerful work we will give you here. But any super-structure needs a foundation; put out the effort to build yours well.

LAYING ON OF HANDS AND SPECIAL GNOSTIC GEMSTONE AIDS TO HEALING

For our first "handle" on more powerful healing work, let's elaborate on the last section of Chapter 6. For a number of years I have taught a simple Gnostic version of healing by the laying on of hands. If not before, at least during the entity building work of Chapter 10 (the lover-attracting entity), you experienced the feeling of real energy flowing out from your hands, and you deliberately controlled the color and so the level of vibration of it. Thus you already have developed the ability to be a pumping station for the healing energy. To work on a loved one or friend is easy. Begin by sending the blue energy between your hands; then starting with your patient's root center, put your strongest hand behind the center and send the energy while willing it to be pulled out through the front of the center with your weaker hand. You will feel the change in quality of the energy as the center is cleansed and flowing freely. Then move to the spleen chakra and do it again, cleaning out each chakra in turn until all seven are flowing freely. Then move to the afflicted area and send the blue energy through there in the same manner to break up the blocks to good flow. When the blue energy is flowing well, change the color you are sending to the life-giving red energy to build up the healthy tissue and energy flow patterns. Five to ten minutes for the complete treatment is generally enough to eliminate the pain and get the patient's natural healing processes started on an accelerated basis for a quick return to normal, healthy functioning of the organ or part.

To work on yourself in this manner requires a bit of adaptation where your arms don't bend in such a way that you can get your strong or sending hand behind a center. Still you can always work to pull the energy out through the front with your weaker or receiving hand until you have coaxed a full flow through the center. One word of caution—ALWAYS wash your hands in cold water when you finish a healing treatment (also *between* healing treatments) to avoid infecting or re-infecting yourself with the negative symptoms you have pulled out of the patient or yourself; and remember, when working on a wound or weak area of the body, use the red energy to put back the life after you have burned away the dross with the blue. This method by itself will bring you many victories.

But we have already commented that the Gnostic lore includes using the power of gemstones, and this is especially useful in the realm of healing and pain relief. A bloodstone placed as near as possible to the center of pain (or a group of small bloodstones clustered around the center of pain) will provide the emanation of a soothing, healing energy which over a reasonably short period of time will reduce or eliminate the pain and enhance the body's normal regenerative and healing processes. The best use of the bloodstone is to first give a treatment with the red and blue energies as we just discussed, then using a hypo-allergenic sheer surgical tape (which you can find in your local grocery or drug store), tape one or more stones in strategic places where the help is needed.

Similarly if an organ or other part of the body is sluggish and needs to be stimulated, a piece of tourmaline taped as close to the area as is reasonably possible should provide it with the needed lift. Or in the case of an overactive organ or super tense condition, there can be a toning down or sedation of the part by application of a piece of rose quartz. Here students of acupuncture or reflexology will quickly perceive a new tool to add to their arsenal. I can only hint at this part of the work here, but I would be happy to discuss it in correspondence with dedicated students. Also, where the physical wearing of the stones would be excessively embarrassing or otherwise impractical, the act of placing them on the appropriate parts of a good photograph of yourself (or your patient), and directing the blue and red energies to them with your hands as you set up the picture, can be almost as powerful—and certainly more convenient.

RESULTS FROM THE GEMSTONES AND
LAYING ON OF HANDS

R.F. gave us this report on her use of the Gnostic healing and gemstone work: "For almost ten years I was what you call a thyroid patient. I had been sluggish and overweight and quite unable to control the weight problem by diet. After a lot of testing my doctor decided I had a major thyroid deficiency, so he put me on thyroid pills. And it certainly helped; I got more energy and with much care I even got some control of my figure again. But there are unpleasant side effects from the thyroid pills and I was unwilling to accept a life sentence of living on the doggone things. When I encountered this part of your Gnostic work, I was enthusiastic about the idea of getting rid of those awful pills. So I started to spend ten minutes twice a day, half in sending blue and the other half in sending red energy through my thyroid or throat center. It did seem to help my energy level, so I was heartened enough to get a good-sized tourmaline which I wore taped to my thyroid area almost 24 hours a day."

"After a couple of weeks, I seemed to be almost hyperactive so I went to my doctor (leaving my stone at home) and asked if I could cut down on the pills. After the examination he told me to cut my daily dosage of pills in half. Again I was encouraged and kept it up, also getting another tourmaline to put on the throat area on a picture of me that I got for my altar. Then on my own I experimented with skipping a day on my pills for a while, and finally got to where I was taking them only twice a week and still feeling just *full* of pep and energy. I continued to cut back slowly until I reached the point where it had been a whole month without a pill and I still felt vigorous and vitally healthy. So I scheduled another examination and at that time told my doctor I had not taken any of the medication for a month. He was as delighted as I at the results of the tests. My thyroid is now completely normal and functioning just right to keep my body in good shape. Now I've been cutting back on the length of time I wear my tourmaline. In another couple of months I expect to be completely normal even without the gemstone. It's really wonderful."

J.E. gave us this interesting report on a different kind of problem: "I have been a chronic migraine sufferer for as long as I can remember—and I can specifically remember headaches that aspirin wouldn't help as far back as when I was five or six years old. Over the years I have consulted regularly with medical doctors and often let them try out the latest drugs and theories on me, but the only thing that seemed to help at all was niacin taken soon enough (when the slightest hint of a migraine appeared). And there are drawbacks to niacin, too, like the itching all over when you get a reaction to it. Then I got into the Gnostic work and of course did the sacrifice ritual for my health improvement, and still use it about once a week. There seemed to be some slight reduction in frequency and severity of the migraine attacks, but they were still coming almost twice a week and lasting 12 hours to three days. In meditation I got a clue that my shoulder and neck muscles could be a source of advance warning so I could start work before the pain in my head got serious. I began to check the tension of these muscles several times a day, and sure enough they always tightened up several hours before an attack. At this point one tends to question cause and effect of parallel symptoms. Anyway, I went to work with the gemstone energy idea to find out. I got some bloodstones for the head, rose quartz for the shoulder and neck muscles and a tiger eye to help protect the solar plexus which seemed to be picking up the tensions that wound up in my shoulders."

"I worked on cleaning my chakras twice a day and began wearing the tiger eye on my solar plexus and some rose quartz on the shoulder muscles in the hollow area above the collar bone where it doesn't show under a shirt. I wore them all the time except in the shower and managed to go two whole weeks almost totally pain free, and when I did get a mild headache I was able to recognize the extra stress pattern that had caused it. So with care I stretched the time before the next problem to a full three weeks. Al, I still slip once in a while, but for all practical purposes I am no longer a chronic migraine sufferer. Now when I get an attack (and they are always very mild and of short duration), I stop and thank my spirit friends for the reminder to live the stress-free life of the Gnostic Magician to preserve my perfect health."

THE GNOSTIC "POWER OF THE INFINITE" HEALING RITUAL

If the regular cleaning of your chakras and the judicious use of gemstone power have not been enough to win for you, the Gnostic "Power of the Infinite" Healing Ritual is clearly indicated. In this ritual we will create a living entity just as we did in the lover-attracting ritual, only this entity will have the sole purpose of breaking up your disease-causing thoughtforms and insuring your perfect health. By now you know that preparations should include the goodies for a brief ritual of joy to set the mood. Beyond this, two blue or red tapered candles, jasmine incense, jasmine perfume oil, a snapshot of you and a small bloodstone will complete your physical preparations, but if you have not yet memorized the health sacrifice affirmation as we gave it for you in Chapter 6, then it would be best to write out a fresh one and take it with you to your altar also.

Open your ritual by lighting your candles and incense and anointing your brow, throat and heart chakras with the perfume oil. Then do a comfortable but brief ritual of joy to get the mood and feeling of contact with the energy transformer personalities just right. Follow this with one clear health sacrifice affirmation. (It is not necessary to burn the paper this time; just get a good feeling of sacrifice of the negatives.)

Now you are ready to begin the work of building the special entity to help you. Speak aloud: "Good spirit friends and energy transformer personalities, it is time to build my perfect health entity. I invite your special help as I start the work now."

Put the snapshot of yourself on the altar, preferably within easy reach but still in a place where you can leave it reasonably permanently. Put the bloodstone on your picture, covering the center of greatest weakness or pain, and announce aloud: "This picture and stone now form the nucleus of power for my perfect health entity."

Then hold your hands close to the picture with the palms facing in, just as we did to build your lover-attracting entity. Focus the root center red energy between your hands and *feel* it forming a big ball of power as you speak, "With Nergal's powerful help, I fill this growing entity with the vitality and sheer regenerative power of the bright red energy."

Shift the focus between your palms to the brilliant orange color and feel this special power being added to your entity as you speak: "Now mighty Ra helps me fill the entity with the wonderful orange energy that burns away all negative emotions as it adds its special clarity of thought and effective reasoning."

Change the color to yellow and feel that fresh power flowing as you speak: "Now my special friend, Ishtar, helps me endow the entity with super intuition and effectiveness.'

Next the green goes in as you speak: "With Osiris' great help, I give the entity strength, courage, love and growth."

Switch to the sparkling electric blue color as you speak: "Marduk helps me bring his special creativity and power to cleanse away any negativity from me or this magnificent entity. My entity is filled with this super helpful energy now."

Then focus the indigo energy as you say: "Thoth helps as I endow my entity with wisdom and the ability to communicate well on both the psychic and material levels."

Finally focus the violet energy as you say: "With Bast's wonderful help I fill my entity with spirituality and spiritual power."

Now you are ready to program the entity. Think beautiful thoughts of the joys of perfect health into the entity, along with special directions to heal any specific weakness or physical problems as you invite the extra power: "I invite the special help of Isis and Abraxas as I complete the programming of my entity. We will call it P.H., standing for *perfect health*. P.H., you are now fully programmed as my perfect health entity. Your sole mission is to bring my physical, mental and emotional beingness into perfect health, then to assist in maintaining that health until it becomes time for me to relinquish the physical body and return to my life in the spirit world. You will thrill with me to the vigor and sheer pleasure of my perfect health, and together we will enjoy life's pleasures and productiveness to the fullest. I will meet with you daily to share a bit of mutual encouragement and be receptive to your guidance and suggestions for a more enjoyable, vigorous and meaningful life, and we will share all of its goodness as partners in happy living. So mote it be."

Sit quietly when you have finished speaking and be receptive to any communication or guidance from your entity, the energy transformer personalities and/or your spirit friends. And when you feel that it is finished, thank all who helped, snuff your candles and go on about your normal activities.

SPECIAL HELP FROM YOUR PERFECT HEALTH ENTITY

There is no limit to the healing help you can bring to yourself through your perfect health entity. K.V. gave us this exciting report: "I've had a perforated eardrum with no hearing in my left ear for years. Finally I decided to use the Gnostic Power of the Infinite Healing Ritual to heal my ear. I enjoyed the work of building the entity (P.H.), and since I live alone I have greatly enjoyed my evening conferences with P.H. I have regularly encouraged him to work on that left ear, and after only three weeks I got my happy results. It happened so naturally—the other day I answered the phone with my wrong hand, so put the receiver to my 'bad' ear, and HEARD EVERYTHING PERFECTLY! I went to the doctor and he says the tissue has grown back and healed the perforation. He also said this 'never' happens. Spirit and my entity are indeed magnificent!"

J.T. reported this way: "I was given a life sentence to the prison of a wheel chair after my accident. The doctors said there was no hope of my ever recovering the use of my legs, and I guess I sort of resigned myself to my fate. So I lived in my rolling prison for over a year before I encountered your Gnostic Magic. It seemed easy to manifest money with the magic, but that was of small consolation to a hopeless cripple, except that it promised a potential of success in other areas. It didn't take long to decide to build my perfect health entity, and it was fun programming it. I pictured us running and jumping and laughing—and enjoying a super sex life again. During those moments that I worked to build the entity and at each of my daily conference sessions with my P.H., I felt a genuine enthusiasm that started from my heart and went upward first as if opening a channel of power. Then I would feel the power pushing itself down my back toward my legs. After just two weeks I noticed I could move my right big toe, even if it was just slightly. This was the encouragement that P.H. and I both needed. The enthusiasm grew in power and the power began a steady regeneration of the nerves and tissues. I left the wheel chair permanently at the three-month point, and today (a month later) I am having a wonderful celebration ceremony of burning my cane. I'm not running and jumping yet, but my sex life is satisfyingly back to normal and I know that I will be 100% physically effective soon. You know that I thank P.H., the energy transformer personalities and my spirit friends many times each day."

SPIRITUAL/PSYCHIC PREVENTIVE "MEDICINE"

We do a lot talking about timing in all of our occult work, but I can think of no instance where it is more important than right here. Obviously it is much harder to program an entity with thoughts and feelings of health and vigor when you are in pain or feeling badly "dragged out." The best time to do the work of building your perfect health entity is when you are already feeling much better than you have for a long time. Even if you are in perfect health, there are still those times when you have that super special sense of well-being. And THAT is the perfect time to begin your Gnostic Power of the Infinite Healing Ritual. But human nature is such that we seldom get well enough motivated to do it. All I can do here is to urge you to spend the time *enjoying* the ritual as soon as you can, and particularly next time you're feeling great. The rest is up to you.

Generally the feedback on this part of the work is singularly unspectacular. My own case is a good example. With one minor exception involving a simple fungus infection and just one trip to the doctor, I have not had *any* medical treatment since about 1954—and I am in better health now than at any time in my life. There is a special vitality and spring to my step and I enjoy every moment of my life. And I am not some sort of freaky exception; that is exactly the way it should be for YOU! But we do have a bit of feedback that will help you understand the value of the preventive ritual work.

S.Y. gave us this very provocative report: "I have pretty generally been in good health all of my life, but since I went through the ritual work to create my perfect health entity, I have enjoyed an extra edge of zest and happiness. I wouldn't have written to you, but I just had a very narrow escape and I feel it may help some of your other students to understand.

"I have a sort of joy session with my entity (I call him P.H. just as you call yours) when I do my basic ritual work at bedtime. The evening in question brought me a very uneasy feeling about going to work the next morning, but I stood my ground and said I'm in perfect health and have a perfect attendance record at work so I'm not about to ruin it by playing hookey tomorrow. There was sort of a reluctant agreement from P.H. so I forgot about it and went on to bed.

"Next day at work I was suddenly KNOCKED to the floor by P.H., and while I lay there wondering what had happened a tank of chemicals exploded right across the aisle from me. If I had been standing up I would have been hit in the face by a caustic solution heated above the boiling point. As it was I got a couple of minor burns on one arm which healed up within a couple of days. Without the help of P.H. I'm sure I would have been at least partially blinded if not killed. Fortunately the fellow who works with me had just bent over to see what was wrong with me, so he escaped with only a couple of second degree burns too. He doesn't understand and thinks we were just 'lucky,' so I'm not about to burden him with the truth. But you can be sure I have had lots of thank-yous for P.H. and for all my spirit friends at my altar. I will be forever grateful that I took the time to enjoy building my P.H."

GNOSTIC MAGIC MIND JOGGERS

1. There is no impossible task for the Infinite, and that certainly includes any necessary healing of your body.
2. Since you are working with the Infinite, to an accomplished Gnostic Magician there is no impossible or incurable condition.
3. Always begin your healing work with the health sacrifice ritual we gave you in our basic health chapter.
4. When the sacrifice ritual is apparently not enough, use the laying on of hands technique and the healing power of gemstones to assist your work. Gemstones are particularly useful in stimulating a sluggish organ or calming an overactive condition.

5. For the more serious conditions, use the Gnostic Power of the Infinite Healing Ritual to build your perfect health entity. Then work with "P.H." to restore your perfect health. Together you can overcome any condition.
6. Preventive medicine is always the least expensive. Build your perfect health entity while you feel wonderful (*before* you *need* it), and work with it to stay in perfect health until it is time to cast aside this body and resume your life in the spirit world.

13

How Gnostic Magicians Win at Games of Chance, Horseraces and Lotteries

Feeling and mood generally combine with a good working knowledge of the game you are playing to make you a consistent winner. We have all heard it said that scared money can't play poker, or in the broader form, "Them as has gets." And we have all jokingly commented that any bank will lend you as much money as you want just as long as you can prove that you don't *need* it. The basic implication from an occult standpoint is that it takes supreme confidence to sense and capitalize on your "hot" streaks, then walk serenely away when you feel it cool off. For many of the gambling games we play, that could well be enough, but for others you will see that some degree of spirit help is essential to winning. We will start with the easy things, then let our momentum carry us on to bigger and bigger victories.

HOW TO SENSE AND CAPITALIZE ON YOUR "HOT" OR WINNING STREAKS

Let me make a "sure thing" bet with YOU right now. I'll bet that you can remember some time in your life when you were motivated to bet on something and you KNEW that you would win, but there was no "rational" way that you could be so sure. Now think of the other times when you faked that feeling to talk yourself into a bet and of course lost. You might say that the difference between the amateur and the professional is just that the pro never fakes that feeling. If it isn't there, he doesn't play. In exactly that sense, this chapter will be a great success if we can use it to make a pro out of YOU. But I have already told you the secret—learn to sense your hot streaks and play them big, then walk or cut back to a token bet when you cool off.

In our psychic development classes at E.S.P. Lab, I often suggest that my students use the horse races for practice in developing the qualifying feeling that lets you know when a hunch or intuitive flash is accurate. The understanding is easy: along with every psychic input, whether intuitive or by some borderline technique or device, there also comes a qualifying feeling. When you learn to recognize that feeling, you KNOW that its input is correct; and without that special feeling the so-called input is nothing more than a random guess. This is one of those areas where there is no substitute for experience—you have to practice and keep at it until you develop the skill and expertise that make you a winner. But there is a special extra bit of fun to the practice periods: while you are learning you know that it is as important to be wrong occasionally as it is to be right. How else could you experience the feeling of the difference?

A simple tool to help you is the classic pendulum. You can make or buy a fancy one, but a piece of thread tied to a weight (say three paper clips or a tiny fisherman's sinker) is as good as the most expensive ones. When your pendulum is ready, first tell it that it is a direct tie to your own preconscious or psychic mind—it will believe you. Next, ask it how it will move to say *yes*, and note the reaction. Then ask it how it will move to say *no*. For most people it will move forward and backward for *yes* and from side to side for *no*, but for others it may move in circles, clockwise and counterclockwise. Once you have established the convention for the communication, tell your preconscious that you want to play the game of predicting the outcome of tomorrow's races. Then read the name of each horse in the first race in turn and note the reaction of your pendulum; also try to remember the *feeling* that came with your positive reactions. Then go on to do several more races, but take care not to spend so much time on it that you get tired or bored. The preconscious has quite a short attention span and must be kept interested in much the same way you must keep the attention and interest of a small child—keep it FUN.

When you get the results in the next day's paper, be sure to compliment your preconscious on its wins, and try to remember the difference in *feeling* between the winning predictions and those that "bombed." As you practice and keep score for several days, you will begin to get a solid understanding of how it works for you. In general you will note that the more you enjoyed the doing of it, in effect the more fun it was for you, the more accurate were your predictions. There is often a brief "honeymoon period" with this part of the work as this report from B.D. indicates: "I went home from class, made my pendulum and tried picking four races as you suggested. Then I went to the track and messed things up a bit. I had all four winners, but because I didn't understand how to bet I only won $50. So I tried it for the following Saturday, too. This time I only had two winners out of the four, so I still only won about $50. Then as you explained I got excited and downright greedy about it, which made me tense and took the fun out of it all. So for a couple of weeks I struck out, not even a show position for any one of my four picks!

"After we discussed it in class again and I understood, I went back to playing at it and now I quite consistently get two or three winners out of my four picks—enough to make a fun trip to the track and with my modest betting bring back at least enough winnings to take a friend and me to dinner at the nicest restaurant I know. I realize that it's best for me to keep this as a fun hobby, otherwise I'd get too tense about it and block myself again."

**GETTING SPIRIT HELP WITH THE GNOSTIC
MAKE-ME-A-WINNER RITUAL**

Some of us can do very well at picking horses or numbers
by just developing that working contact with the preconscious or subliminal part of ourselves. Others will need a
big boost from their spirit friends. And ALL of us need spirit
help in the big lotteries or any other major sweepstakes or
games where you have nothing to say about the number you
get so that effective precognition will not help you. Let's add a
word of caution here before I explain the power of the
Gnostic-Make-Me-a-Winner Ritual. Lotteries and sweepstakes attract occultists and magicians like a dairy atracts
flies—in countless multitudes! Picture one of the big lotteries
where the odds against you are a million or more to one. Now
let's say that your magic is really good and cuts those odds all
the way from a million to one down to a thousand to one. We
would agree that that is powerful magic, but if you still don't
win, and at a thousand to one the chances are still slim, you
have no way of knowing how truly effective your magical
work really was. When you don't win the big ones, it is not a
cause for discouragement, but a time to be more selective in
picking the place to play. It's better by far to win three or four
hundred dollar prizes than to miss on the million dollar one.
This is not to say don't enter the big ones, but to suggest that
you keep your perspective and find the ones that you CAN
beat consistently to develop more of the feeling and attitude
of the winner and so give yourself better and better chances of
winning the big ones also.

With that in mind let's turn our attention to the Gnostic-
Make-Me-a-Winner Ritual. If ever there was a time to stress
the fun element in our work, this is it. So naturally the
preparations should include the goodies for a ritual of joy. Also
you will need green or blue tapered candles, a good frankincense or prosperity incense, and frankincense, prosperity or
power perfume oil. The final preparation is to write out your
spirit invitiation sheet in your own handwriting. It should
read: "Nergal, Ishtar, Marduk, Bast, in the spirit of good

fellowship and fun, I ask your special help. Let me be a winner in all areas of my life, and in particular let me win [*here insert a brief description of your specific request, e.g., 'the Pennsylvania lottery,' or 'at poker with my friends tonight.'*] My loving thanks to you for the joy of feeling like a winner."

To begin your ritual, light your candles and incense, and anoint your brow, throat and heart centers with your perfume oil. Then have a short but really fun ritual of joy. Use the feeling of oneness and happiness you generate as the power to win in the rest of the ritual. When you are ready, fold the spirit invitation sheet between your palms as you picture yourself in a shaft of bright white Light. Feel the happy Light energy flowing through you and charging your sheet with joyous life, then read it happily aloud for six times before you touch it to your candle flame and read it for the seventh time just ahead of the flame. Drop it into your prepared receptacle, then sit quietly but happily to see if there are any bits of inspiration or instruction for you from your spirit friends or the energy transformer personalities. When you feel that it is finished, thank your friends, snuff your candles and go back to your normal routine.

I.T. gave us this report on his use of the ritual: "Last February I started using the Gnostic Make-Me-a-Winner Ritual and I kept on winning small lotteries throughout the whole month to a total of just over $1,000. Then I guess I got busy and forgot about it for a while, but when I started using it again in June, I again won over a thousand dollars. Now I'm on a kick of using it regularly to see if I can increase the monthly winning total."

T.N. reported this happy experience: "After just about a month of regular use of the Gnostic Make-Me-a-Winner Ritual, I got on the game show, 'Concentration,' and won a brand new Chevrolet!"

And C.B. shared this experience with us: "I got invited on a spur-of-the-moment trip to Las Vegas. There wasn't time to do the Gnostic Make-Me-a-Winner Ritual, so all I could do was throw the bare essentials into my bag and take off. Naturally we started to gamble almost as soon as we arrived, and I wasn't doing well at all. Between Keno and the slot machines I had lost about $60 when I decided it was time to go to the room and regroup. I didn't have candles or incense, but I had put in some power oil, and I decided to make do with what was at hand and try at least a rinky-dink ritual. I wrote out my spirit invitation sheet on the back of a Keno ticket and used a 7UP for the ritual drink. When I finished the ritual and was sitting quietly with my eyes closed, I saw a counter spinning. It stopped at 4, then ran on and stopped at 32, and ran on again and stopped at 76, then it just faded away. I wrote down the numbers and realized that it was for the Keno. Right then I said, 'OK, good friends, I know you mean to help, but I get bored at the Keno. I'll play the three spot, but no more than five times.' So back to the casino I went and put a dollar on the three numbers. I lost, so I kept my promise and played again, and lost again. The third time I got two of the three numbers which just gave me my dollar back. Then the fourth time I lost again. When I got up to bet the fifth time I said quietly, 'OK, guys, you got me one free ride and this is the last play, so I'll bet two dollars.' And I hit! I got back $84 and was ahead! So I went back to the slot machines and got three nice jackpots within 45 minutes. I wound up the trip over $200 ahead—the first time I ever had a winning trip to Las Vegas!"

HOW TO MAKE AND USE YOUR GNOSTIC MAKE-ME-A-WINNER LUCKY MEDAL

Now let's talk about carrying your good luck with you. Down through the ages everything from a rabbit's foot through a four-leaf clover to a myriad of amulets, talismans and medals have been carried by millions of people for good luck. If you probe deeply enough into the private life and possessions of even the most staunchly three-dimensionally logical person, you'll find a lucky penny or shoe, or some object that he cherishes unobtrusively as something of a personal good luck charm. Our Gnostic work is naturally not an exception. It comes with the very powerful idea that an amulet or medal ceremonially made and personalized for you can, by its presence on your person, bring the same sort of extra power that you get for the first few moments or hours after doing a highly successful Make-Me-a-Winner Ritual.

Timing is especially important in this part of the work. Take care that you do not engage in any part of the making or activation of your Make-Me-a-Winner Lucky Medal after a full moon. All of this is to be done while the moon is waxing (after the new moon and before the next full moon). If you can also take care to see that the moon is in a fertile sign you will add even more power—but if you're not sure about that part, let your basic feeling or sense of timing guide you to the exact starting time. Figure 1 is a drawing of the Make-Me-a-Winner Lucky Medal before it has been personalized. Then Figure 2 is the same medal, but after it was personalized for me. Here caution is in order: DO NOT CUT FIGURE ONE OUT OF THIS BOOK or deface it in any way; that would destroy its potential usefulness to you. Here is how you should go about making your own (see page 184):

A small piece of parchment paper of thin wood (or if you're good at metal working, a thin piece of copper, silver, etc. will do fine) will serve as the basic raw material. For a pattern, a silver dollar is just the right size. Using permanent ink, trace around the silver dollar to make a neat circle. Next, copy Figure 1 as neatly as possible inside your circle, taking care to leave enough room for your signature (as in Figure 2) in the middle. You will naturally not do a perfect job, but even the imperfections will help to make the medal uniquely part of you, and so more effective for you. After the activating ritual, I glued my Make-Me-a-Winner Medal to a silver dollar, then coated it with clear fingernail polish for protection—but that's the way I felt about it; let your own esthetic senses guide you in that area. Just plan to have it in a form you can easily have with you in a pocket or purse at all times when the element of luck is involved in your activities—or if you're like me, you'll keep it with you at all times just on general principles, like who knows when you might need it!

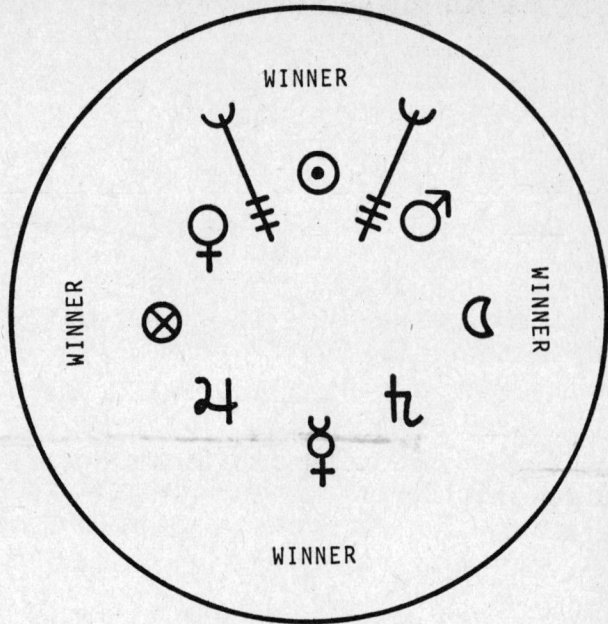

FIGURE 1

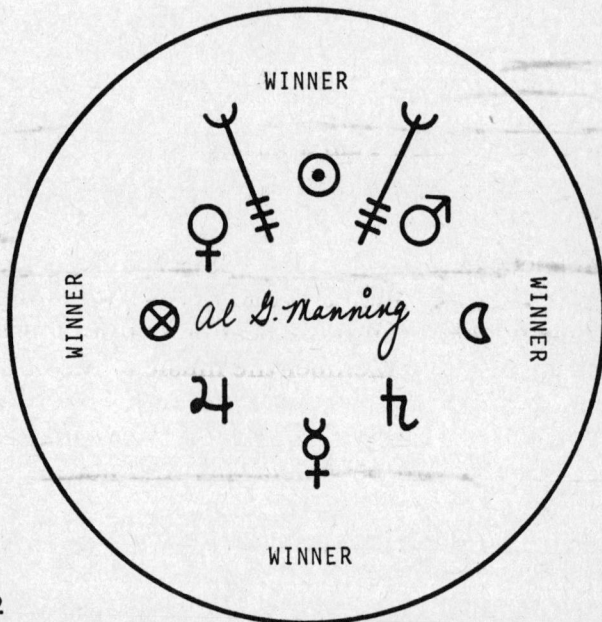

FIGURE 2

HOW TO ACTIVATE YOUR GNOSTIC MAKE-ME-A-WINNER MEDAL

The medal activation ceremony should come at the end of a fresh Gnostic Make-Me-a-Winner Ritual. Prepare as always for the very happy bit of ritual work, and take your Make-Me-a-Winner Medal with you to your altar also. As you finish the chanting of the spirit invitation sheet and drop its ashes into the receptacle, pick up the medal and hold it between the palms of your hands. Again feel the lovely white Light flowing into you and through your hands into the medal. While you hold the medal, picture first red, then orange, then yellow, all the way up your chakras until you end up with the eighth (red violet) color on the eighth use of the activating chant:

> A winner, a winner, a happy Gnostic winner,
> Please help me charge my medal now, I am a
> winner anyhow.
> A winner, a winner, a happy Gnostic winner.
> A winner, a winner, a happy Gnostic winner,
> My thanks to all forevermore; I'm happy as
> I score and score.
> A winner, a winner, a happy Gnostic winner,
> and I know I am a winner evermore.

Imagine the colors as best you can, but don't be too particular about that part. The real power to this chant comes from the rhythm and meter. When I was watching this, my spirit people hooked it into the beat of a rather loud clock. If you're old enough to remember the music of the 40's and the 50's, think of it as kind of a boogie beat and really swing it. The more the chant comes out like really moving music, the greater power you will be generating. And nothing is to say you can't start back with the red and go up again (and again) if you're enjoying yourself. Again this is one of those times where the more you enjoy it, the more power it brings you. Then when you feel it is finished, relax for a few moments to give your spirit and/or energy transformer personality friends a chance to reach you with fresh ideas or inspiration. And when you feel ready, thank all your friends, snuff your candles and go back to your normal routine. But take your Make-Me-a-Winner Medal with you and keep winning! Does the medal ever need recharging? Yes, anytime it feels weak to you, or at least once a month—say the night after the new moon.

HOW WELL DOES IT WORK?

Many of my best bits of feedback on the use of the medal were told to me in strict confidence by people whose success was so outstanding that the story would clearly identify them. But we'll share the ones we can with you here. D.J. reported: "I did the Gnostic Make-Me-a-Winner Ritual with my son to help him charge up his Make-Me-a-Winner Medal. I also gave him a bottle of power oil to help. We had lots of fun singing the chant and felt plenty of power going into his medal. Then he applied to and got on Hollywood Squares. He got the secret square and wound up winning well over $10,000! And we both know that that is just a happy start for his new life of a regular winner!"

This one has to be slightly sketchy because I promised to carefully protect the identity of this person whom you would otherwise easily recognize: "For the past several years I've averaged between $50,000 and $75,000 a year by freelancing in my chosen profession. Since my tastes are simple, I've never felt any lack on the personal level, but there were some business things I wanted some extra money for. So I decided to try the Gnostic Magic on a lottery with a first prize of $25,000. The ritual work is always fun, and I particularly enjoy the beat while my spirits and I are singing the activating chant for my Make-Me-a-Winner Medal. I had three weeks to wait for the drawing, so I had a partial ceremony every night— as much for the fun of playing with my spirit friends as anything. I wanted to win, of course, but I was completely relaxed about it because it clearly was not a matter of survival for me. Then I guess my spirit friends were a trifle disappointed because we only took second in that lottery, $10,000 instead of the $25,000, so they arranged a 'consolation' prize for me. Two days after the drawing I got an offer of a 'part-time job' in my field doing something I've always wanted to do. It takes about four hours a week and doesn't interfere with my other income-producing efforts (except to gain me more prestige, so it will help), and I'm guaranteed an extra thousand dollars a week for doing it—with a potential in the serious fractions of a million annual income if I want to expand it later. I'm sure you understand why I have avoided much detail and asked that my name and profession be withheld, but I wanted to share as much as I can so your other students will be sure to recognize the full potential of the work."

GNOSTIC MAGIC MIND JOGGERS

1. The first principle of winning at gambling games is to develop your ability to sense and exploit your "hot streaks," then back off when you "cool off."
2. There is a feeling that comes with and qualifies a good psychic input. Only practice will teach you to consistently recognize that feeling.
3. Make a simple pendulum and use our horserace prediction exercise to easily get the experience in a fun way. Remember it's as important to be wrong once in a while as to be right, so you can experience the feel of the difference and so learn to fully qualify your inputs.
4. Many people can learn to do good predictive work with just the pendulum as a tie to their own preconscious or subliminal mind.
5. If the pendulum exercise doesn't work well for you, or in situations where you have so little control that precognition will not help you (as in lotteries and sweepstakes), you need definite spirit help. Use the Gnostic Make-Me-a-Winner Ritual.
6. Make and activate your Gnostic Make-Me-a-Winner Medal and carry your good luck with you permanently.

14

The Special Fun of Gnostic Magic — Levitation, Astral Projection, Invisibility, Bi-Location

Picture a big business executive on the golf course, tennis court, or squash or handball court. Watch him find reserves of physical and instinctual energy in the name of fun that would bring out-and-out rebellion if he were required to expend them at the office. If you will think about it, you will realize that the main difference between work and fun is that for the same amount of energy expended you tend to be tired from work, but exhilarated from fun! This will help you to understand my big stress on fun and playing at the work that we find as the unifying thread through all of the Gnostic Magical lore.

I sincerely hope that you are learning to interject more and more fun into everything you do, and that you already see how much extra energy and effectiveness it gives you. But this book would surely not be complete without a brief sojourn into the real play area of Gnostic Magic. There are practical benefits to most of this fun, too, but the real value is in the recharging of your emotional and spiritual batteries in the joy of play. Let's look at ways to share more of this life-giving fun.

LEVITATION—YOUR SPIRIT FRIENDS AT PLAY

There is probably no more practical justification to levitation than climbing a mountain "because it's there." And to spend months or years striving to develop a technique for this is not at all appealing to my practical nature. But I have been aware of the phenomenon for many years, as attested by this little episode in 1953 when my wife was in the process of "dragging" me to a party I was not keen on attending. When I threatened to levitate and spend my whole time at the party on the ceiling, her spontaneous response was: "So go ahead and I'll just say loudly, 'Al, you come down from there, I've told you a thousand times that's not funny.'" And over the years in my class work, I have encountered many instances of spontaneous levitation.

This is not the sort of book where it would be appropriate to give you an elaborate set of disciplines and rituals for levitation, where the practical value would come only if you happened to fall off a cliff. But it is important to recognize the possibility that it may happen to YOU spontaneously—so you can enjoy this special experience without its being marred by fear. To me a spontaneous levitation is a combination of a pat on the head and a reminder from your spirit friends of the total power of the unseen. I can guarantee you a fresh feeling of AWE when your feet once more touch the floor and there is time to digest the experience. In the astral work we will discuss in a moment, there are games where a group of spirits may well toss you back and forth between them like a volley ball, and I tend to relate the gentle levitation of your physical body to the same thing—your spirit friends at play. If it happens to you, just remember to enjoy it and happily accept the gift and the lesson from your playful friends.

THE GNOSTIC MAKE-ME-INVISIBLE RITUAL

Have you ever wanted to sneak up on a friend? Or just go somewhere and not be noticed? If you will remember, the occult power of becoming invisible was demonstrated on several occasions by Jesus in the New Testament of the Bible, and he certainly left us the challenge, "These works that I do shall ye do also, and greater works shall ye do...." This is definitely one of the occult "tricks" that is best learned on the fun level, but once learned it can be used to extricate yourself from many a sticky situation.

The classic old radio program, "The Shadow," spoke of the power to cloud men's minds so that the Shadow became invisible, and it was based on solid occult truth. In my class work there are times in just about every session where the aura of one or more students becomes so strong that the physical body is quite invisible. And if you use a mirror for mediation, I'm sure you have experienced a few times when your image faded away. (We use this as a technique for seeing your faces from past lives at times also, but I've given that a good deal of treatment in other books.) But enough for the feasibility study; let's get to the "how to."

This is a case of doing the groundwork when you don't need the power, so that it is available when the impish desire to become invisible strikes you, or when it would be pleasant to avoid someone who is coming right at you. The technique is like the "key word" idea in self-hypnosis, simply programming your preconscious mind so that when you speak the phrase, "Make me invisible now," there will be complete compliance from all the necessary parts of your beingness and you will pass unnoticed to the place you want to go. A mirror on your altar is essential for this part of the work, and the only other preparation is for our classic ritual of joy. When you have finished your ritual of joy, speak aloud:

"Good friends, I invite your help in programming my preconscious to quickly respond to my request to make me invisible for a reasonable period of time. With your helpful instruction, my preconscious can instantly learn the necessary adjustments to make in my aura to let me go unseen. With your happy help, let's practice now."

Then sit quietly and stare at your face in the mirror. After a minute or more, say, "O.K., preconscious, make me invisible now." All the while keep staring at your image in the mirror, expecting to see it fade away to darkness or nothing-ness. When you see it fade away, wait for half a minute or so, then say, "O.K., let's bring me back to normal visibility," and watch as your image reappears. It's quite reasonable to add an extra measure of fun to this part by occasionally inviting a face from a past life to appear instead of your own, but the emphasis should be on getting your own image to fade and reappear on call. Once you get the feeling well in hand, you should be able to use it in the "real world." Try it just for fun and to further develop the ability. Use it to walk up and stand right next to a friend before you decide to appear and be noticed, and keep practicing so that when you reach a time when you "really need it," the skill is there for you.

Since this is a "fun chapter," I'm not going to give you examples; rather all of this is my challenge to YOU to get your own outstanding results, then send the reports to me for our research files—and (as those of you who are familiar with the work of E.S.P. Lab know) for inclusion in the regular competition for our "Magician of the Month Award."

MOST FUN AND GAMES OF GNOSTIC MAGIC ARE FOUND IN ASTRAL PROJECTION

In almost all of our work so far we have in effect invited our spirit friends to come over to our house to play. Now it's time to accept the invitation to go to your spirit friends' houses to play with them in their own back yards.

Yes, it is quite natural to take virtually all of your awareness and most of your consciousness out of your body in order to effortlessly visit distant places on earth, or better, to visit places in the astral and spirit world where you can never take your physical body. To me this latter part is the only real value of astral projection. With enough practice, the tech-niques of our last chapter can take you to look at anything in the world, past, present or future, but it will not be much help in experiencing from the spirit point of view. And what sort of friend would we be if we insisted that our friends ALWAYS come to our house and refused to ever pay a return visit?

Aside from the ideas of courtesy and reciprocity, there are very special personal benefits from astral projection. When you are out of your body, the touch and hug from a spirit becomes much more real and very special. I could write a whole book on the joys of astral sex, but we will touch this only very gently here—this is not the place to earn an X rating.

If ever the basic Zen ideas of direct experience were in point it is right here. In Zen, the classic discussion goes that you can spend pages and pages of writing trying to describe an apple, but all that writing is virtually meaningless to a person who has never tasted one. The Zen practitioner will tell you that the only way to understand an apple is to bite into it. And certainly that is true of astral projection work. We can prattle about it forever, but it will mean very little to you until you generate or recognize an astral experience of your own. So let's head right into the playground of the Gnostic Magician, the astral world.

In the ancient Egyptian traditions, the aspirant reached a certain level of progression where it became necessary to his further development that he have a conscious astral experience. At this point it was the responsibility of the priest (or hierophant) to hypnotize the aspirant, lift him out of his body, then leave his own body and conduct the aspirant to the places of learning on the "higher planes." The Gnostics naturally carried this the next step forward in convenience, so we find your spirit lover or teacher taking the place of the physical hierophant to assist you in leaving your body and take you on a safe trip to friendly and educational places on the other side of the veil. This gives you a good idea of what is to come next, so let's get right at it.

USING THE GNOSTIC ASTRAL PROJECTION RITUAL

This is another time when the most important part of the preparation is YOU. If you are tense and anxious, you will find yourself effectively "locked into" your physical body. The only way to get out is to produce the separation through relaxation and gentleness. Physical preparation should include a very big, comfortable chair, if possible—one that your physical body won't fall out of when you leave it. The alternative is a nice bed, but if you're lying down there is too great a tendency to drift off to sleep before the separation, and so perhaps to have the experience without the full conscious control that makes it best.

Begin at your altar with a nice ritual of joy, then invite your spirit lover or teacher to come with you to the big chair (or bed) to be there to greet you as you float out of your body. Settle comfortably into the chair, take a few slow deep breaths, check the key tension muscles of your body (neck, shoulder, back and leg muscles) and deliberately relax them. A bit of rubbing or massage with your own hands will usually help. The idea is to be as completely relaxed as possible. Now if you see aura, look for the aura of your spirit lover in front of you waiting for you to come out. If you have not yet developed good aura vision, just picture your spirit lover there. Then harness your creative imagination to feel that you are getting lighter and lighter as you relax more and more, all the while breathing very slowly and deeply. Keep getting lighter and lighter until you feel yourself able to float right up out of your physical body. As you feel yourself coming out, reach out your hand and feel your spirit lover take it to reassure you that all is well. If the feeling of separating from your physical body frightens or excites you, it will have the effect of popping you right back in, and it will take several minutes of slow breathing and relaxation before you can do it again. But you *can* get out with patience and practice.

If by chance you don't make the full conscious separation on your first few tries, when you are ready to conclude the work, ask your spirit lover to wake you up on the astral next time you are asleep. Often your first few clearly astral experiences will come in that way, either spontaneously or because you tried to do it consciously and asked to be awakened out there as a follow-up to your efforts. For more background and alternate methods of out-of-the-body travel, you will find a chapter on this work in almost all of my previous books, in particular *The Miracle of Universal Psychic Power, Miracle Spiritology,* and *The Magic of New Ishtar Power*

My files are full of feedback on astral experiences, but since this our fun chapter I want to challenge you to get me some feedback of your own. Many of the feedback letters I have already received involve some pretty "way out" experiences of astral classrooms and instruction, or X-rated discussions of how nice it is to enjoy astral sex with one's spirit lover at his (or her) astral house, but there are practical applications, too. Take care to be ethical and not just a plain old "snoop" with your early astral work. But it's often fun to snoop a little for the purpose of "spooking" a good friend who you know will not be too shocked by your teasing.

The basic characteristics of what we normally call an astral projection or trip are the traveling of your consciousness from place to place in a form that looks exactly like the aura of a spirit being or entity (except that you remain attached to your physical body by the silver cord). You are aware of your surroundings, and the colors are much more vivid than in the three-dimensional world, but people in physical bodies generally are unaware of your presence, and you are quite unable to affect material things. For instance, you can't turn on a water faucet because your hand goes right through it; and of course you don't have to look for a door, you simply walk right through the walls. This is an ideal situation for eavesdropping or flat-out espionage, but I trust that your personal ethics will preclude that sort of shoddy practice.

THE PHENOMENON OF BI-LOCATION

In constrast to a normal astral projection is the much more rare but still fairly common phenomenon most often called bi-location. In this condition, you appear to be completely physically present in two or more separate physical locations simultaneously. The German word, *doppelganger,* has been adopted into the English language (I checked and found it in my dictionary) as about the closest term we have for the condition. In general the disciplines involved to produce this manifestation fall into the same category as those for physical levitation—outside of the scope of this book. But since this so nicely reflects my Gemini personality, and because it may well happen to YOU spontaneously, it is worthy of a few lines of consideration.

Have you ever had a friend accuse you of walking past him (or her) on the street and snubbing him by not responding to his greeting, but you KNOW that you were somewhere else at that exact time? True, your friend may have been mistaken, but equally possible is the fact that you were experiencing a spontaneous manifestation of bi-location *without* being fully conscious in both bodies. The spontaneous version of this phenomenon generally has you appear in a distant city or distant part of your city from where "you really are," and sometimes even carry on an intelligent conversation with people while you're there—all with NO CONSCIOUS MEMORY on your part. Reminds you a bit of the classic Red Skelton character who always said, "Boy, a flock of 'em flew over that time," doesn't it?

Of course the disciplined and fully developed manifestation literally gives you the often-dreamed-about ability to be fully functional in two places at the same time; we've all felt the need for that at one time or another. If this is of really burning interest to you, I have a solid suggestion: first develop the ability to slip in and out of your physical body to visit with your spirit lover, teachers and friends; then ask them to take you to the proper classes on the astral where you can be taught to do it.

This is a place where my feedback files are quite sparse, so I would particularly appreciate a feedback letter from you if ever you produce a good manifestation of this phenomenon. Meanwhile, if a friend insists that you were somewhere you know you were not, don't be quite as adamant as you otherwise might; just pass it off with, "Oh, that must have been my doppelganger you saw," and avoid an argument. Besides, that could be the perfectly correct explanation.

GNOSTIC MAGIC MIND JOGGERS

1. Levitation of the physical body is a fact, the disciplines for which lie outside the scope of this book. We mention it because there may be times when your spirit people become playful or excited and do it to you. Don't be upset, ENJOY it.

2. Whether from Biblical or legendary authority, we know that the power to pass unnoticed from place to place (generally described as invisibility) is fact. With practice, *you* can learn to do it. Do the ritual work in advance so that when you need the ability, you are already programmed to achieve it.

3. Astral projection has been handed down to us in tradition from the ancient Egyptian times, where the priest or hierophant used hypnosis to lift the aspirant out of his body, then accompanied him to the instructional work in the spirit planes.

4. Think of this as a "Goody, can I come to your house to play" ritual and let yourself float out of your body to take the hand of your spirit lover or teacher.

5. The possibilities of special learning situations and highly practical information-gathering from your astral trips are endless. Learn as you enjoy.

6. The phenomenon known as bi-location is differentiated from astral projection by the fact that you are seen as if in a physical body in two or more locations simultaneously. The disciplines to achieve this can be learned from your spirit friends in classes on the astral. We mentioned it here primarily because you may experience spontaneous manifestations of the phenomenon with less than full memory and it may help you to understand these otherwise confusing situations.

7. I have deliberately left the feedback out of this "fun chapter" as a special challenge to you to generate your own set of personal experiences and write about them to me in your own feedback letter. (I will give my address at the end of the last chapter.)

15

How to Be a Master Gnostic Magician — Complete and Secure in All Ways

There is always a touch of nostalgia for me when we reach this point in a book. Here I must wrap it all up into a solid and useful program for you and once more take my leave. This book has been an often thrilling and always uplifting experience for me. The months of research beginning with my many trips into the past to observe the usages, then the experimental presentation of the basic principles to a special few who tried them with me, and finally putting it into what I hope you will agree is simple, modern English, all served to build a feeling of special camaraderie not just with those who experimented with me, but with each of you who will read this book. I feel a special friendship for each of you that I hope will extend on in time at least for the balance of this earthly sojourn. We will end this book with an invitation to you to make our friendship closer and more personal, but first we must be about our important business of setting things in order with an overview of perspective and purpose for you.

YOUR LIFE MISSION IS TO BECOME
A TRUE MASTER

I could give you six or eight volumes of philosophical arguments about the meaning and purpose of life, but the practical man must be slightly skeptical of the mental gymnastics of philosophy; like physical gymnastics, they may be good for conditioning, but they never get you anywhere. Instead of trying to use a bunch of arguments to sell you something, I will continue to present the things I've learned in my research and experimentation, with the idea that you already accept my pragmatic approach that if the principles produce positive and useful results for you they are true—at least until we find a new set of principles that work better.

There was a sneaky purpose behind that last bit of discussion—it illustrated the practical process of growth (or better, evolution). On the scientific level, mankind "accepts" a truth because it seems to be supported by experimental fact. It finally becomes a scientific "law" and those who disagree with it are thought of as fools. For a thousand or more years before Columbus, a man was considered an idiot if he believed that the world was other than flat. Then more complete experimental evidence was introduced and the scientific world adopted the new truth that the world is a spheriod, and soon even the idea that it is the earth that revolves around the sun, not vice versa. Before the days of extensive exploration, the notion of a flat earth was as useful as any other, just as before interplanetary exploration it mattered very little on the practical level which body orbited which. But as growth (or evolution) marches along, we must continually be prepared to cast off our old, limited ideas in favor of new, less limiting truths, which may in time have to be cast aside for even better ones.

How does all this apply to you? In exactly the same way. You are totally confined and limited by your current set of beliefs. I hope that makes you quite comfortable for now, but as you live on it is important to your healthy progress that you be completely willing to cast aside even your most cherished beliefs in favor of new ones which are proving to be more accurate and useful. All of which brings us to your meaning and purpose in life. An infinite number of theological and philosophical answers are offered to you as potential beliefs, but one stands out (at least to me at the moment) as the most practically useful and comfortable of the lot. It is simply that you were sent to this classroom we call earth life to learn and grow until you become a true Master. And very little reflection is required to figure out that the things you do in the direction of furthering your evolution bring you progress and personal satisfaction, while the detours make you miserable in one way or another.

We recognize that we are part of nature, so nature's purpose should be supportive of our premise if it is correct. And what do we see of nature's purpose except the constant improvement of each species by the inevitable (except in the case of man himself) process of natural selection, otherwise called the survival of the fittest. Man is unique only in that his powers of self-conscious thought, observation and reason allow him to understand this process; but *that alone* is enough to lift YOU above the laws of natural selection. How? By simply following the old adage, "If you can't lick 'em, join 'em," and deliberately setting up a plan of cooperation with the evolutionary forces. Then don't just follow it, but strive regularly to improve it.

SETTING YOUR PERSONAL LIFE PLAN TO GROW INTO FULL MASTERSHIP

To build a plan for growth, we must first assess the situation. Where are we now, what tools do we have to help us, and what is standing in our way? And if you seem to have more than your share of handicaps, don't complain—they may well be advantages which will save you from the many distractions that so often hold back the others. This is a race of a different sort, where to reach the goal is victory, but everyone who reaches it before you paves the way for *you* to win, too! The only losers are the ones who don't try, or who become mired in the distractions along the way.

Let's recognize that to be a Master means that you are in complete command of your physical, material, emotional and spiritual existence. Thus the steps toward Mastership will certainly improve your physical and economic lot as well as your emotional comfort and spiritual awareness. In all of the literature and instructions that have been handed down to us over the ages, there are booby traps set up by insecure priests and teachers to deliberately hold us back lest we become greater than they. And to an even greater extent, the modern "educational process" is really a system of brainwashing to see that the student accepts all the limitations imposed upon him as the price of fitting into society. So that in truth, the path to Mastership lies not so much in learning more, but in recognizing and discarding those limiting concepts and "laws" that have acted as unseen chains to stifle your development.

The heaviest chain of all is the careful programming we have received since childhood to take ourselves too seriously. Lincoln set the proper tone at Gettysburg with the classic line, " The world will little note nor long remember what we say here. ... " And it also cares very little what we do here; success or failure is an intensely personal thing, best measured by your own standards. Although we can be sure that the world doesn't care about you, we know just as surely that you are not alone—there is great interest and care for YOU from your spirit lover and guides, the energy transformer personalities, and through this link, from DEITY itself. Indeed, the very hairs on your head are counted, as the Master taught 2,000 years ago, but we must keep a perspective that delegates the worry and importance to spirit, leaving you free and unfettered to play the game of growth happily and victoriously.

True, you may run into the Vedantic teaching of *Maya* which says that even this precious thing called growth is an illusion. And there is a way in which that is completely true, but growth is still the only game in town and it's far better to play than to mope on the sidelines. We should go right about mastering the final ritual of this work, but there is one small point to consider first. The great teachers or avatars of all the world's major religions would quite properly be called "Masters" because it was out of their demonstration of Mastership over things of this earth that their teachings gained the wide acceptance it takes to be called a major religion. But this Mastership was clearly and in all cases not a loner's or egotist's trip. Each in his own way demonstrated the application of the power by attunement with the higher forces of nature that we call spirit or spiritual.

The energy transformer personalities with which we have communed in this book are your direct link to the primal spiritual forces of the universe. They could just as well have chosen to be called by the names of a set of Christian or Hebrew angels or stations on the tree of life, but they preferred to manifest for us in the more totally non-sectarian and universal form, using less familiar names from ancient and now extinct cultures lest they be limited in their appeal to just one third of the earth's population. So I can safely assure you once more that this powerful Gnostic work is completely compatible with your present religion and with any religion that you may choose to adopt in the future.

THE GNOSTIC GROWTH RITUAL

It would be an excellent plan to use this ritual about once a month, say on each new moon, for the rest of your sojourn in this earthly body. This is really an advanced version of the basic ritual of joy, and the preparations are the same. Two green tapered candles, a bit of frankincense or love/prosperity incense, and jasmine or power perfume oil will be just right, along with your choice of brandy, wine or grape juice, and almonds or other low calory munchies. Try to set a happy party mood as you light your candles and incense and anoint your brow, throat and heart centers with with perfume oil. Picture yourself bathed in a shaft of bright and loving white Light, and greet your friends: "Good friends—energy transformer personalities, my spirit people, and nature spirits—

welcome to my growth ritual party. Let's have a wonderful time together."

Then lift your glass to Nergal, have a sip, lift a morsel of food to him, and take a small bite. Focus your attention on your root center and speak aloud: "Brother Nergal, it is a joy to share food and drink with you. Now as I am focused on your energy center, I ask your help not just in making it strong, but in your suggesting the ways I can best assist you in promoting my growth and progress."

Repeat this action for Ra, Istar, Osiris, Marduk, Thoth and Bast in turn, pausing for whatever seems to be the right length of time between them. Then toast Isis and Abraxas together and invite their guidance and help. Finally, toast your spirit lover, guides and friends and the nature spirits, and invite their help and guidance also. Then sit in silence in the glowing party mood and let your thoughts drift where they will, knowing that in this way your friends from the other side have the best opportunity to get their ideas and guidance through to you. When you feel that it is finished, thank all your friends for coming, snuff your candles, and go quickly to make notes on the ideas you have received. (Alternatively, you may have brought pad and pencil to your altar, but to most of us that would feel much too businesslike for a party.)

Feedback from the Gnostic Growth Ritual usually looks like this one from Shirley S.: "I honestly felt that I was doing fine, but you said we should do the Gnostic Growth Ritual on each new moon, so I decided to try it. From Nergal I got a feeling that I was still too inhibited and unresponsive in my sex life. Ra reminded me of a minor conflict with a co-worker and suggested a simple and tension-removing solution. And Osiris pointed out a couple of areas where I was slightly taking advantage of my husband's good nature. I took the advice to heart and acted on it—and you wouldn't believe the difference! Suddenly there's a whole new dimension of wonder and fulfillment in the bedroom (and wherever else we get the urge!); my work situation is happily more comfortable since I got rid of the small conflict; and my marriage is magnificent! I don't know whether being more considerate of my husband improved our sex life, or my resolve to be more responsive in the bedroom made us both more considerate of each other. But who cares! It's delicious. And I got a nice raise at work, too! With this much really unexpected good from the first one, you can be sure that I'll be faithful to the regimen of a growth ritual at each new moon. Viva!"

The growth ritual will work its own miracles for *you*, too. Use it to spot your obstacles and negative trends, then use all the techniques and rituals we have given you in this book to grow over, under or around *any* obstacle. *You can do it*, and I would certainly like to hear from you about your successes in the process!

We spoke of making a personal life plan for your growth to Mastership, but I deliberately saved it until after the Gnostic Growth Ritual. After all, you will get the best suggestions for your growth during and after the ritual. Then you need some degree of organization of your plan. At least mentally, list your projects in the order of their importance and set time goals for their progress or completion. You will find it of great value to write down your list, then save it for six months before you get it out to update it—this is literally giving yourself your own report card. And no one else could be more interested or better qualified to do it.

HOW TO BE SURE THAT YOU WILL LIVE THE GOOD LIFE FOREVERMORE

Once more it's time to face life "like it is." Human nature is such that you have one last major hurdle to get over on your way to gaining full and permanent control over your ever-improving life. Our Gnostic Magic has presented you an effective and highly practical system to make every part of your life richer, fuller, and more fun as you tread the happy path to Mastership. But all too many of my readers will say, "That's right, and I'm going to try it one of these days," then set the book on the shelf and forget about it. Don't let that be YOU!

Another group of readers will do better. They will enthusiastically try the ritual work and get very good results, but along the way they will become so interested in their new things and situations that they forget what caused their good fortune. So in time they will slip back into the old ways and find themselves in trouble again. I hope this won't be YOU, either.

You do know that there is a better way which guarantees you regular progress and freedom from major setbacks. It is to stay in tune with your spirit friends and energy transformer personalities by working with them, if only a few moments EACH DAY, on projects that promote your personal growth. But not many keep it up alone. If you have time to participate in a local magical or occult group, you will find that the sharing of ideas and experiences with others of reasonably like mind helps keep you stimulated and challenged to grow more. And I want to add a suggestion to supplement your local group work (and/or any other group work you may be doing), and at the same time allow me the pleasure of deepening our personal friendship. I need your "feedback" reports to stimulate my next research projects, as well as to suggest troubleshooting methods if you are not getting the magnificent results we both know you should. I carry on this part of my work through E.S.P. Laboratory, a nonprofit religious/educational corporation, in Los Angeles. The Lab is a fun group with members living quite literally all over the world. We encourage each other's progress by regularly sharing experiences and research results through the monthly newsletter. I would like to introduce you to E.S.P. Lab as one more way to maintain your progress without forgetting what is promoting it. But most of all I want to hear from you about your experiences as you apply yourself to the happy rituals of the Gnostic Magic and move ever more joyously forward on your path to Mastership.

So I happily invite you to write me at the following address, and let's continue to share the fellowship of growing *together*!

Al Manning
c/o E.S.P. Laboratory
7559 Santa Monica Boulevard
Los Angeles, CA 90046

GNOSTIC MAGIC MIND JOGGERS

1. On the scientific and practical levels, the thing called truth is constantly evolving. If we are to grow, we too must be ever ready to give up an old truth in order to accept a new and more useful one.
2. We can look to nature to find the purpose of life. The lesson we see is evolution (growth and improvement) of each species by the process of natural selection (the survival of the fittest).
3. We human beings have a similar purpose, but we are unique. Our ability to recognize and enter into the process of evolution gives us the power to transcend the dangers to an individual of natural selection—by cooperating in our growth.
4. Don't complain about your handicaps. Let them be assets as you set a sound program to grow into personal Mastership.
5. Use the Gnostic Growth Ritual at least on each new moon to get the fresh guidance and direction that will keep you on the path of ever more wonderful success.
6. Don't be one who loses because you didn't try, and avoid slipping back because you forgot what was causing your progress and good.
7. Regular contact with others of like mind will help you stay happily on your path of growth. Participate in local groups if you can. And do write me about your progress and invite me to tell you more about our work at E.S.P. Lab. I'll look forward to deepening our personal friendship.